*This book belongs to:*

**LEISURE ARTS, INC.**
Little Rock, Arkansas

## EDITORIAL STAFF

*Vice President and Editor-in-Chief:* Anne Van Wagner Childs. *Executive Director:* Sandra Graham Case. *Editorial Director:* Susan Frantz Wiles. *Publications Director:* Carla Bentley. *Creative Art Director:* Gloria Bearden. *Senior Graphics Art Director:* Melinda Stout. PRODUCTION — *Managing Editor:* Susan White Sullivan. *Senior Editor:* Andrea Ahlen. *Project Coordinators:* Carol Bowie Gifford, Jennifer S. Potts, and Stephanie Gail Sharp. DESIGN — *Design Director:* Patricia Wallenfang Sowers. EDITORIAL — *Managing Editor:* Linda L. Trimble. *Associate Editor:* Terri Leming Davidson. *Assistant Editors:* Tammi Williamson Bradley, Robyn Sheffield-Edwards, and Darla Burdette Kelsay. *Copy Editor:* Laura Lee Weland. ART — *Book/Magazine Graphics Art Director:* Diane M. Hugo. *Senior Graphics Illustrator:* Stephen L. Mooningham. *Graphics Illustrators:* Fred Bassett and Faith R. Lloyd. *Photography Stylists:* Pam Choate, Sondra Daniel, Karen Hall, Aurora Huston, Courtney Frazier Jones, and Christina Myers. PROMOTIONS — *Managing Editors:* Tena Kelley Vaughn and Marjorie Ann Lacy. *Associate Editors:* Steven M. Cooper, Dixie L. Morris, and Jennifer Ertl. *Designer:* Dale Rowett. *Art Director:* Linda Lovette Smart. *Production Artist:* Leslie Loring Krebs. *Publishing Systems Administrator:* Cindy Lumpkin. *Publishing Systems Assistant:* Susan M. Gray.

## BUSINESS STAFF

*Publisher:* Bruce Akin. *Vice President, Marketing:* Guy A. Crossley. *Marketing Manager:* Byron L. Taylor. *Print Production Manager:* Laura Lockhart. *Vice President and General Manager:* Thomas L. Carlisle. *Retail Sales Director:* Richard Tignor. *Vice President, Retail Marketing:* Pam Stebbins. *Retail Marketing Director:* Margaret Sweetin. *Retail Customer Service Manager:* Carolyn Pruss. *General Merchandise Manager:* Russ Barnett. *Vice President, Finance:* Tom Siebenmorgen. *Distribution Director:* Ed M. Strackbein.

## CREDITS

PHOTOGRAPHY: Ken West, Larry Pennington, and Karen Shirey of Peerless Photography, Little Rock, Arkansas; and Jerry R. Davis of Jerry Davis Photography, Little Rock, Arkansas. COLOR SEPARATIONS: Magna IV Color Imaging of Little Rock, Arkansas. CUSTOM FRAMING: Nelda and Carlton Newby of Creative Framers, North Little Rock, Arkansas. PHOTOGRAPHY LOCATIONS: The Empress of Little Rock Bed and Breakfast, Little Rock, Arkansas, and the homes of Carl and Monte Brunck, Dr. Dan and Sandra Cook, Nancy Miller, and Duncan and Nancy Porter.

Library of Congress Catalog Number 96-78949
International Standard Book Number 0-8487-4158-7

# INTRODUCTION

As the Yuletide's festive finery emerges all around us, we revel in the glory of the holiday and ponder ways to hearken that spirit into our own homes. More than simply adorning the evergreen, we wish to extend the magical celebration through every hall, to every room. Inside this treasury of hand-stitched heirlooms, you'll not only find traditional holiday decor such as beautiful ornaments and stockings, but you'll also discover a wonderland of nostalgic designs for bestowing joy to every setting. As family and guests step through the doorway, they'll be welcomed by a wintry wreath and heartwarming holiday keepsakes. A stunning illustration of Santa with a host of heavenly helpers will warm the living room mantel, while idyllic images of the benevolent saint will bring cheer to the family room. Enliven your Christmas kitchen with clever accessories, and set a delightful tone for dining with an array of musical motifs. As your family settles in for a long winter's nap, they'll rest contentedly amid dreamy adornments for the bedrooms and bath, as well. On the night before Christmas, may these splendid displays impart peaceful tidings to every creature — all through the house!

# TABLE OF CONTENTS

# home sweet holiday

**W**hether traveling across the miles or across the street, there's no other feeling like coming home for the holidays. As loved ones gather once again, we reunite amid the hugs and laughter that chase away winter's chill. Part of the joy that's shared by all comes from remembering family milestones and celebrating Christmas traditions.

Charts on pages 75-77

# WARM WELCOME

**T**he holidays are a festive time
for opening our homes to friends
and neighbors. As they arrive, we greet
our guests with tempting aromas and
resplendent decorations that reflect the
glory of the season. And as our visitors
depart, we send them off with heartfelt
wishes and a keepsake ornament
from a special hallway tree.

Charts on pages 48-51

9

# LOVELY LIVING ROOM

**F**estooned with elegant hand-stitched trims, your living room will come alive with the miracles of the season. From the top of the tree to the fireplace mantel, we find Santa and a host of angelic assistants preparing for the Christmas celebration. A wonderland of lacy snowflakes, sprinkled upon the tree and around the room, completes the scene with wintry grace.

Charts on pages 52-61

11

Chart on pages 54-55

Charts on pages 56-57

*E*mblems of the holy season
are all around — a benevolent
St. Nicholas, frosty snowflakes,
and heavenly angels. Whether
simple or elaborate in design,
such images surround us
with gentleness and peace.

Chart on page 61

Chart on pages 58-59

Chart

Charts on pages 60 and 61.

A *few well-placed accents spread Yuletide cheer to every corner of the room. St. Nick tops a gilded box, and wintry angels bear woodland gifts for your home. Enhancing an elegant afghan, the merry olde gent is escorted by a legion of cherubs as he begins his grand journey.*

Chart on page 57

Chart on pages 54-55

19

# DELIGHTFUL DINING

**I**nspired by the classic carol "The Twelve Days of Christmas," this elegant collection for the dining room abounds with the splendor of the season. Festive motifs from the song spread cheer about the room, from the tabletop to the tiny tree on the sideboard. These exceptional accents — including our decorative bottle bag — will lend a merry tune to holiday entertaining.

Charts on pages 62-66

Charts on pages 62-63

23

Charts on pages 62-65

24

Chart on page 66

Lovely table linens, including a table runner, breadcloth, and napkins, are lyrical accessories for a holiday meal. Favor guests with old-fashioned Christmas crackers filled with surprises. Assorted candles wrapped with hand-stitched stanzas provide a luminous centerpiece.

Chart on page 66

Charts on pages 62-65

# FESTIVE FAMILY ROOM

*Father Christmas, Kris Kringle, Pére Noël, Sinterklaas — these are the names that children from around the world have whispered when speaking of the benevolent fellow we know as Santa Claus. Each figure, whether clad in crimson and fur or woodland robes, stirs youthful anticipation within us all. You can bring that spirit of merriment to young and old alike by filling the family room with portraits of the jovial gent.*

Charts on pages 68-74

*h*e spoke not a word, but went straight to his work,
And filled all the stockings; then turned with a jerk,
And laying his finger aside of his nose,
And giving a nod, up the chimney he rose.

— CLEMENT CLARKE MOORE

Chart on page 68

30

Charts on pages 68-70

*J*olly old St. Nicholas,
Lean your ear this way!
Don't you tell a single soul
what I'm going to say;
Christmas Eve is coming soon;
Now, you dear old man,
Whisper what you'll bring to me;
Tell me if you can.

— TRADITIONAL VERSE

Chart on page 70

Charts on page 74

Chart on pages 72-73

33

Charts on pages 68 and 70

*As we recall the tradition of St. Nicholas' annual visit, we are reminded of the generosity and goodwill that he represents. It is that gentle essence that inspires us to honor Christmas throughout the year, in all that we do.*

Chart on page 71

# BEAUTIFUL BEDROOM

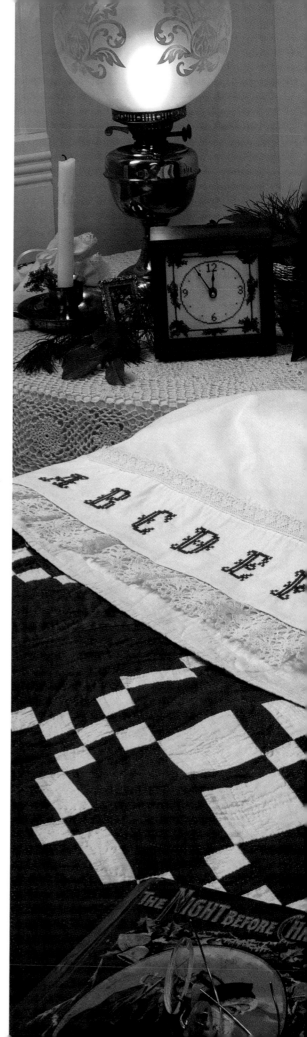

**A**ccented with lovely Yuletide trims, your bedroom suite will become a tranquil refuge in which to enjoy personal holiday moments. Take time to reflect on the peace of the season, relaxing upon embellished sheets, which are too charming to put away when the season ends. Let the gentle image of St. Nicholas be a reminder of the tender blessings the season holds.

Charts on pages 82-87

*T*he holly and the ivy,
when they are both full grown,
of all the trees that are in the wood,
the holly bears the crown.

— TRADITIONAL CAROL

Chart on page 86

Chart on page 87

Chart on page 82

Pamper yourself with an array of luxurious accents, including a beautiful basket of sensuous soaps, as well as holly-trimmed towels and sachets. Endearing Alpine samplers convey glad tidings.

Chart on page 86

Charts on pages 83 and 86

40

Charts on pages 84-85

# youthful yuletide

$\mathcal{B}$eneath the light of the Yuletide moon, Santa embarks on his magical journey, gleefully fulfilling good children's wishes. He whisks from home to home as little ones slumber, slipping down chimneys with ease. In a wink, the jolly elf fills each merry stocking, then pauses to enjoy the sweet treats left for him.

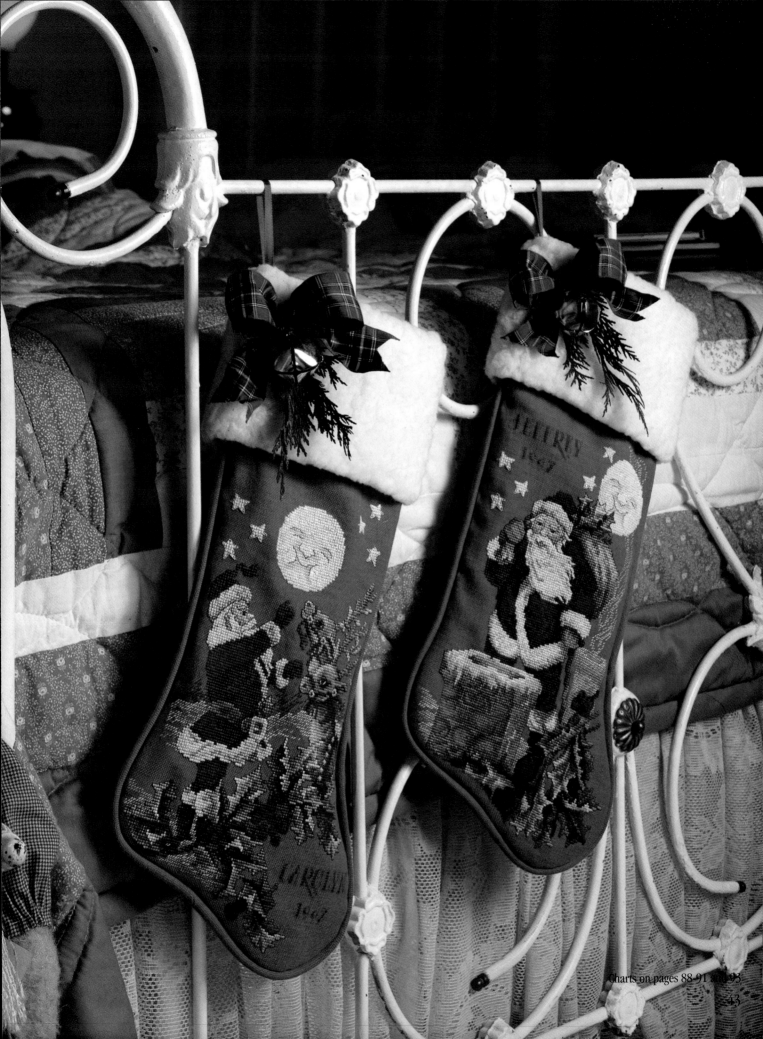

Charts on pages 88-91 and 93

# CHEERY CHRISTMAS KITCHEN

As the tantalizing aromas of cinnamon and nutmeg waft from the oven, we sense that Christmas is indeed near. Tasteful gifts created with loving hands are scattered about the countertops, and gleeful accents fill the room with cheer. Each handmade token reminds us that the joy we bring to others is joy brought back to us.

Charts on pages 78-80

45

*M*y gifts are very little,
But still I always know,
That what I make for those I love
Will true affection show.
Sometimes I sew some little thing,
Or make a candy treat,
But in each case I put in it
A Christmas thought that's sweet.

— AUTHOR UNKNOWN

Chart on page 80

Charts on pages 78 and 80

46

Chart on page 79

As we create festive favors and delicious dinners, we're delighted to find jolly kitchen accessories at our fingertips. A welcoming wish invites dear friends to enjoy the holiday preparations.

BACK DOOR GUESTS ARE BEST

Chart on page 79

63w x 50h

The best thing to give a friend is your heart

| X | DMC | 1/4 X | B'ST |
|---|---|---|---|
| ● | 319 | ◢ | ◪ |
| + | 320 | ◢ | |
| ◎ | 347 | ◢ | |
| ◆ | 367 | ◢ | |
| △ | 368 | ▢ | |
| ☆ | 772 | | |
| | 814 | | ◪ |
| ✦ | 815 | ◢ | |
| | 986 | | ◪ |
| ▦ | 987 | ◢ | |
| ■ | 988 | ◢ | |
| ▢ | 989 | ◢ | |
| ▣ | 3021 | ◢ | ◪ |
| – | 3328 | | |

**Friendship Ornaments** (shown on page 8): Each design was stitched over 2 fabric threads on an 8" square of Cream Belfast Linen (32 ct). Two strands of floss were used for Cross Stitch and 1 strand for Backstitch.

For each ornament, you will need an 8" square of Cream Belfast Linen for backing, 10" x 5" piece of adhesive mounting board, tracing paper, pencil, 10" x 5" piece of batting, 18" length of 1/4" dia. purchased satin cording with attached seam allowance, and clear-drying craft glue.

For pattern, fold tracing paper in half and place fold on dashed line of pattern; trace pattern onto tracing paper. Cut out pattern; unfold and press flat. Draw around pattern twice on mounting board and twice on batting; cut out. Remove paper from one piece of mounting board and press one batting piece onto mounting board. Repeat with remaining mounting board and batting.

Referring to photo, position pattern on wrong side of stitched piece; pin pattern in place. Cut stitched piece **1" larger** than pattern on all sides. Cut backing fabric same size as stitched piece. Clip 1/2" into edge of stitched piece at 1/2" intervals. Center wrong side of stitched piece over batting on one mounting board piece; fold edges of stitched piece to back of mounting board and glue in place. For ornament back, repeat with backing fabric and remaining mounting board.

Beginning and ending at top center of stitched piece, glue cording seam allowance to wrong side of ornament front, overlapping ends of cording. Matching wrong sides, glue ornament front and back together.

*Designs by Linda Culp Calhoun.*

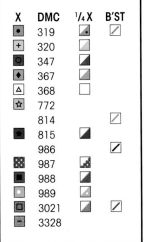

# WARM WELCOME

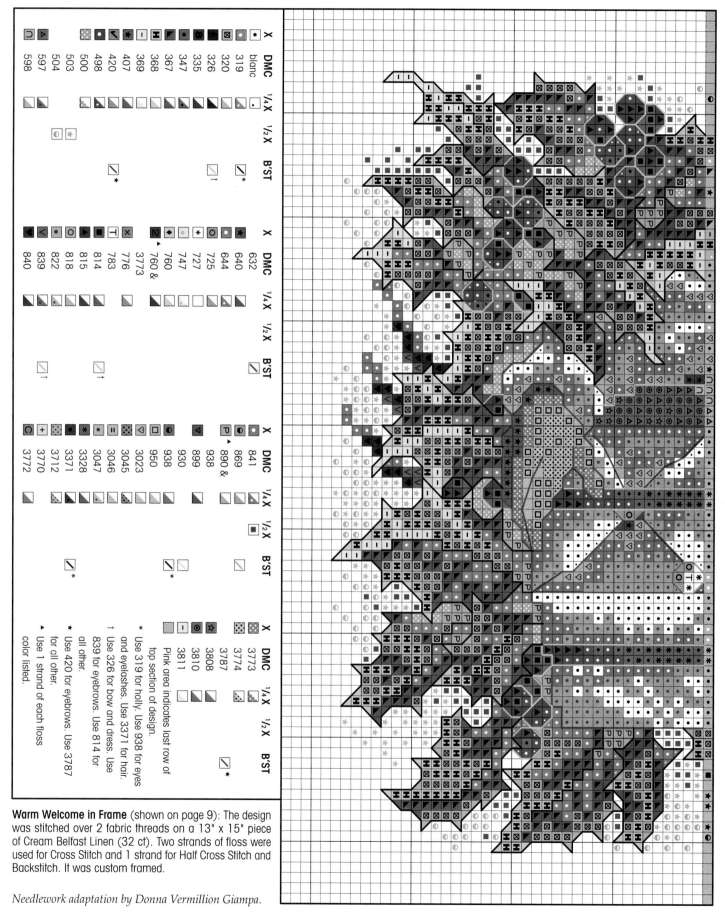

Pink area indicates last row of top section of design.

\* Use 319 for holly. Use 938 for eyes and eyelashes. Use 3371 for hair.

† Use 326 for bow and dress. Use 839 for eyebrows. Use 814 for all other.

★ Use 420 for eyebrows. Use 3787 for all other.

▶ Use 1 strand of each floss color listed.

**Warm Welcome in Frame** (shown on page 9): The design was stitched over 2 fabric threads on a 13" x 15" piece of Cream Belfast Linen (32 ct). Two strands of floss were used for Cross Stitch and 1 strand for Half Cross Stitch and Backstitch. It was custom framed.

*Needlework adaptation by Donna Vermillion Giampa.*

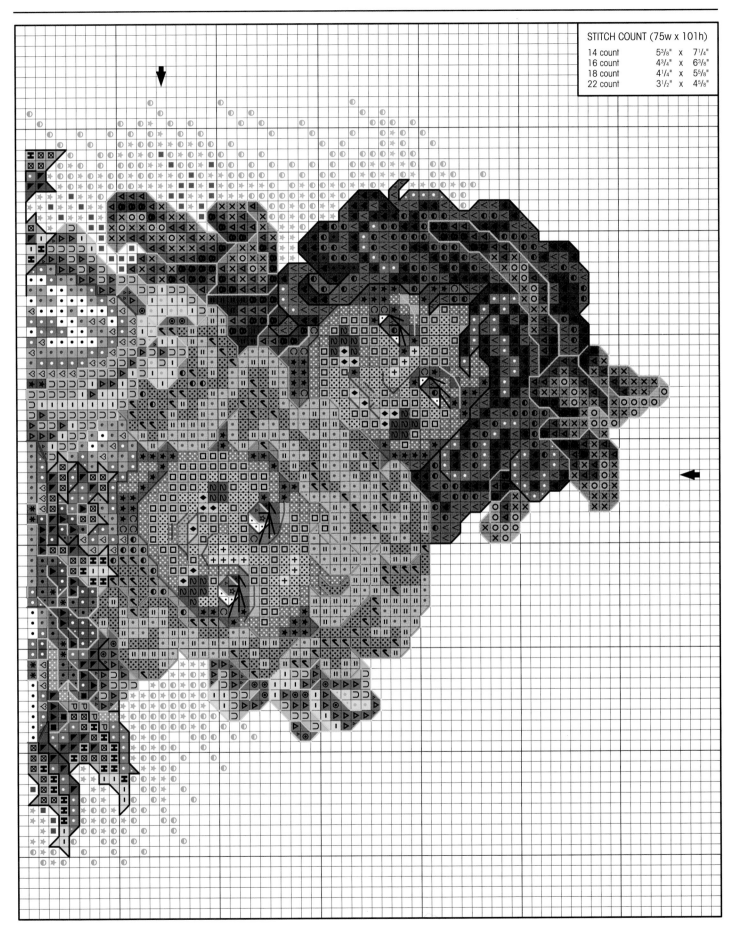

STITCH COUNT (75w x 101h)

| count | | | |
|---|---|---|---|
| 14 count | 5³/₈" | x | 7¹/₄" |
| 16 count | 4³/₄" | x | 6³/₈" |
| 18 count | 4¹/₄" | x | 5⁵/₈" |
| 22 count | 3¹/₂" | x | 4⁵/₈" |

# LOVELY LIVING ROOM

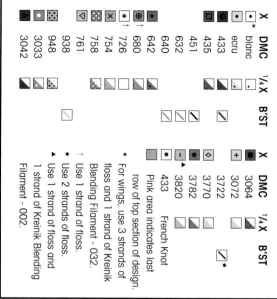

| X | ¼X | B'ST | DMC | X | ¼X | B'ST | DMC |
|---|----|------|-----|---|----|------|-----|
| | | | blanc | | | | 3064 |
| | | | ecru | | | | 3072 |
| | | | 433 | | | | 3722 |
| | | | 435 | | | | 3770 |
| | | | 451 | | | | 3782 |
| | | | 632 | | | | 3820 |
| | | | 640 | | | | 433 French Knot |
| | | | 642 | | | | |
| | | | 680 | | | | |
| | | | 726 | | | | |
| | | | 754 | | | | |
| | | | 758 | | | | |
| | | | 761 | | | | |
| | | | 938 | | | | |
| | | | 948 | | | | |
| | | | 3033 | | | | |
| | | | 3042 | | | | |

Pink area indicates last row of top section of design.

\* For wings, use 3 strands of floss and 1 strand of Kreinik Blending Filament - 032.
→ Use 1 strand of floss.
★ Use 2 strands of floss.
▶ Use 1 strand of floss and 1 strand of Kreinik Blending Filament - 002.

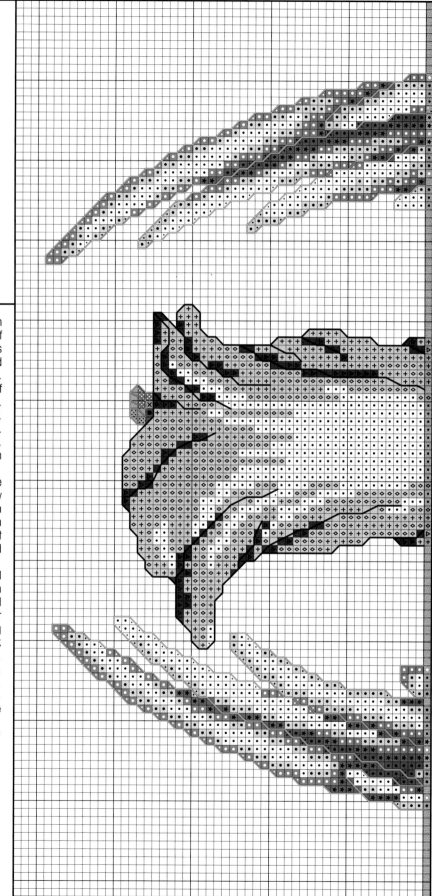

**Angel Treetop Ornament** (shown on page 10): The design was stitched over 2 fabric threads on an 11" x 13" piece of Antique White Cashel Linen® (28 ct). Three strands of floss were used for Cross Stitch and 1 strand for Backstitch and French Knots, unless otherwise noted in the color key.

For treetop ornament, you will need an 11" x 13" piece of Antique White Cashel Linen® for ornament backing, 12" x 18" piece of adhesive mounting board, tracing paper, pencil, 9" x 12" piece of batting, 34" length of ¼" dia. purchased satin cording with attached seam allowance, clear-drying craft glue, and two 18" lengths of ¼"w ribbon for hanger.

For pattern, lay stitched piece on flat surface and place tracing paper over stitched piece. Referring to photo, draw oval-shaped pattern approximately ½" larger than design on all sides; cut out pattern. Draw around pattern twice on mounting board and once on batting; cut out. For ornament front, remove paper from one piece of mounting board and press batting piece onto mounting board.

Referring to photo, position pattern on wrong side of stitched piece; pin pattern in place. Cut stitched piece 1" larger than pattern on all sides. Cut backing fabric same size as stitched piece. Clip ½" into edge of stitched piece at ½" intervals. For ornament front, center wrong side of stitched piece over batting on mounting board piece; fold edges of stitched piece to back of mounting board and glue in place. For ornament back, repeat with backing fabric and remaining mounting board.

Beginning and ending at bottom center of stitched piece, glue cording seam allowance to wrong side of ornament front, overlapping ends of cording. Matching wrong sides, glue ornament front and back together.

For ties, fold each ribbon length in half and tack center of each length to back of ornament 4" apart (**Fig. 1**).

**Fig. 1**

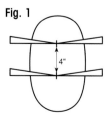

4"

*Needlework adaptation by Jane Chandler.*

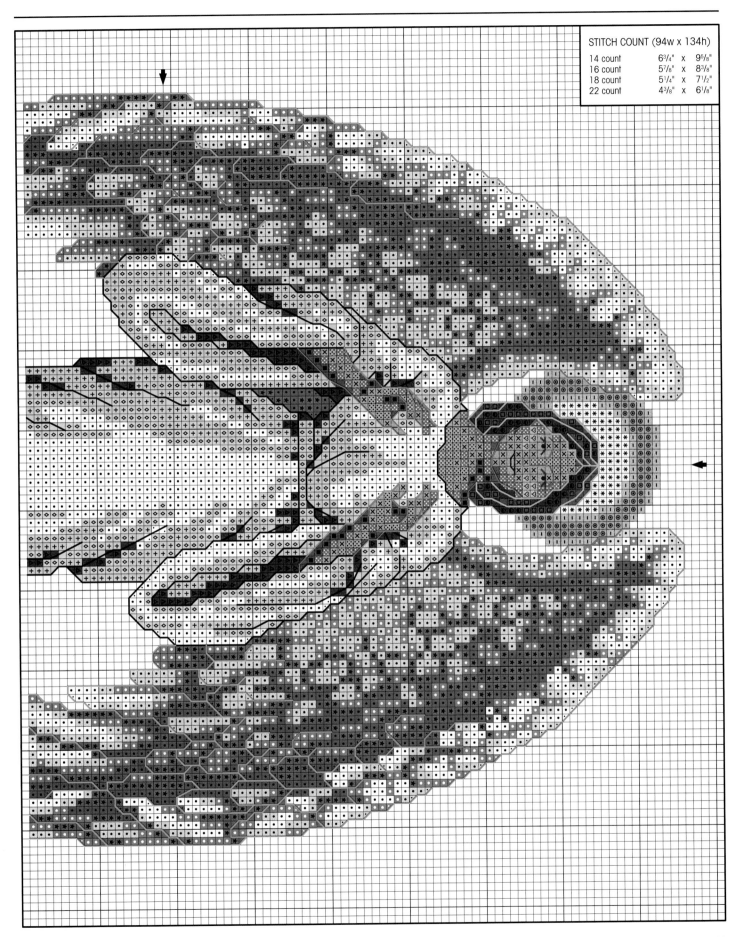

STITCH COUNT (94w x 134h)

| | | | |
|---|---|---|---|
| 14 count | 6³/₄" | x | 9⁵/₈" |
| 16 count | 5⁷/₈" | x | 8³/₈" |
| 18 count | 5¹/₄" | x | 7¹/₂" |
| 22 count | 4³/₈" | x | 6¹/₈" |

# Lovely Living Room

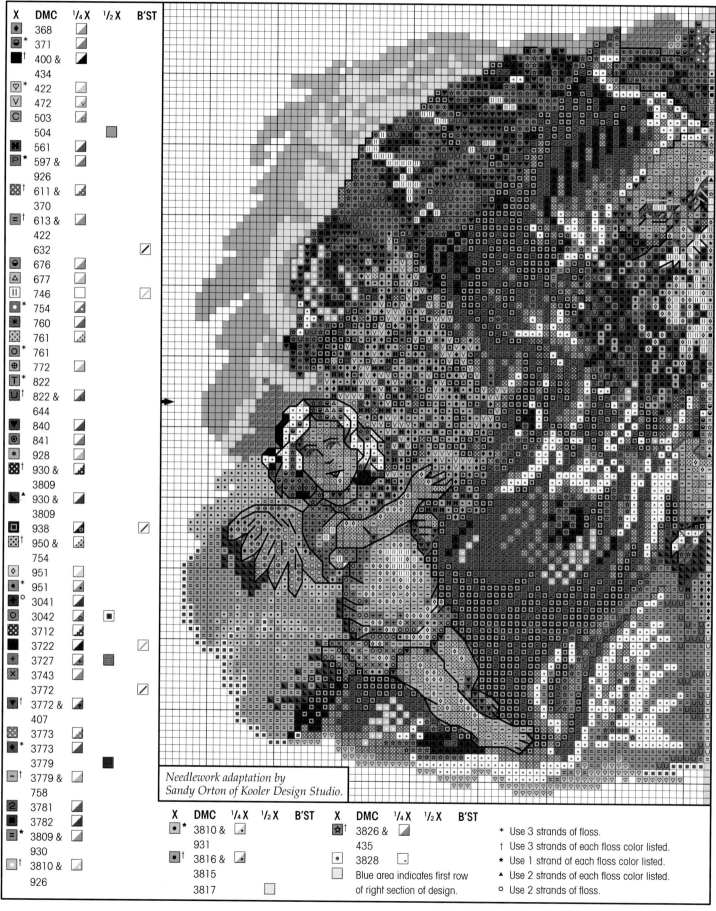

| X | DMC | ¼ X | ½ X | B'ST |
|---|---|---|---|---|
| ◆ | 368 | | | |
| ◉ * | 371 | | | |
| ■ † | 400 & 434 | | | |
| ♡ * | 422 | | | |
| V | 472 | | | |
| C | 503 | | | |
| | 504 | | | |
| H | 561 | | | |
| P * | 597 & 926 | | | |
| ⊠ † | 611 & 370 | | | |
| = † | 613 & 422 | | | |
| | 632 | | | ⟋ |
| ⊖ | 676 | | | |
| △ | 677 | | | |
| ‖ | 746 | | | ⟋ |
| ⊡ * | 754 | | | |
| ✱ | 760 | | | |
| ⬚ | 761 | | | |
| O * | 761 | | | |
| ⊕ | 772 | | | |
| T * | 822 | | | |
| U † | 822 & 644 | | | |
| ▼ | 840 | | | |
| ◉ | 841 | | | |
| ✳ | 928 | | | |
| ⊠ † | 930 & 3809 | | | |
| ◼▲ | 930 & 3809 | | | |
| ◘ | 938 | | | ⟋ |
| ⊠ † | 950 & 754 | | | |
| ◇ | 951 | | | |
| ⬤ * | 951 | | | |
| ◆° | 3041 | | | |
| ⊙ | 3042 | | ◼ | |
| ⊠ | 3712 | | | |
| ◼ | 3722 | | | ⟋ |
| ✚ | 3727 | | | |
| ✕ | 3743 | | | |
| | 3772 | | | ⟋ |
| ▼ † | 3772 & 407 | | | |
| ⊞ | 3773 | | | |
| ◆ * | 3773 | | | |
| | 3779 | | ◼ | |
| ⊟ † | 3779 & 758 | | | |
| 2 | 3781 | | | |
| ◼ | 3782 | | | |
| ⊟ ★ | 3809 & 930 | | | |
| ⬚ † | 3810 & 926 | | | |

| X | DMC | ¼ X | ½ X | B'ST | X | DMC | ¼ X | ½ X | B'ST |
|---|---|---|---|---|---|---|---|---|---|
| ⬤ * | 3810 & 931 | | | | ★ † | 3826 & 435 | | | |
| ⬤ † | 3816 & 3815 | | | | • | 3828 | | | |
| | 3817 | | ⬚ | | | Blue area indicates first row of right section of design. | | | |

* Use 3 strands of floss.
† Use 3 strands of each floss color listed.
★ Use 1 strand of each floss color listed.
▲ Use 2 strands of each floss color listed.
° Use 2 strands of floss.

*Needlework adaptation by Sandy Orton of Kooler Design Studio.*

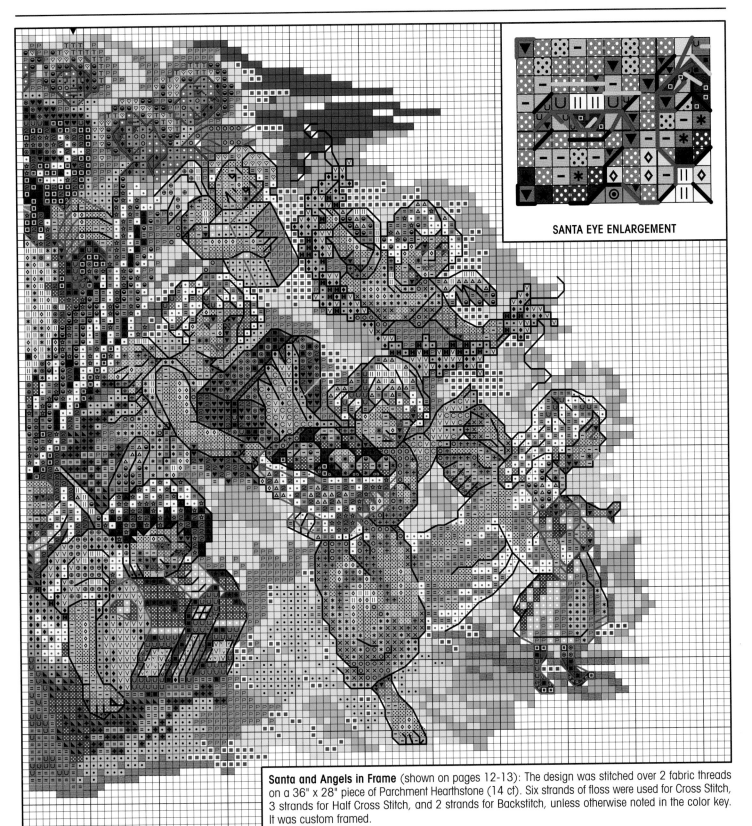

**SANTA EYE ENLARGEMENT**

**Santa and Angels in Frame** (shown on pages 12-13): The design was stitched over 2 fabric threads on a 36" x 28" piece of Parchment Hearthstone (14 ct). Six strands of floss were used for Cross Stitch, 3 strands for Half Cross Stitch, and 2 strands for Backstitch, unless otherwise noted in the color key. It was custom framed.

**Santa and Angels Afghan** (shown on page 19): The design (refer to Diagram, page 57, for placement) was stitched over 2 fabric threads on a 45" x 58" piece of Country Flax Anne Cloth (18 ct). Six strands of floss were used for Cross Stitch, 3 strands for Half Cross Stitch, and 2 strands for Backstitch, unless otherwise noted in the color key. For afghan, see Finishing Instructions, page 57.

| STITCH COUNT (169w x 111h) | | |
|---|---|---|
| 14 count | $12^{1}/_{8}$" | x 8" |
| 16 count | $10^{5}/_{8}$" | x 7" |
| 18 count | $9^{1}/_{2}$" | x $6^{1}/_{4}$" |
| 22 count | $7^{3}/_{4}$" | x $5^{1}/_{8}$" |

# Lovely Living Room

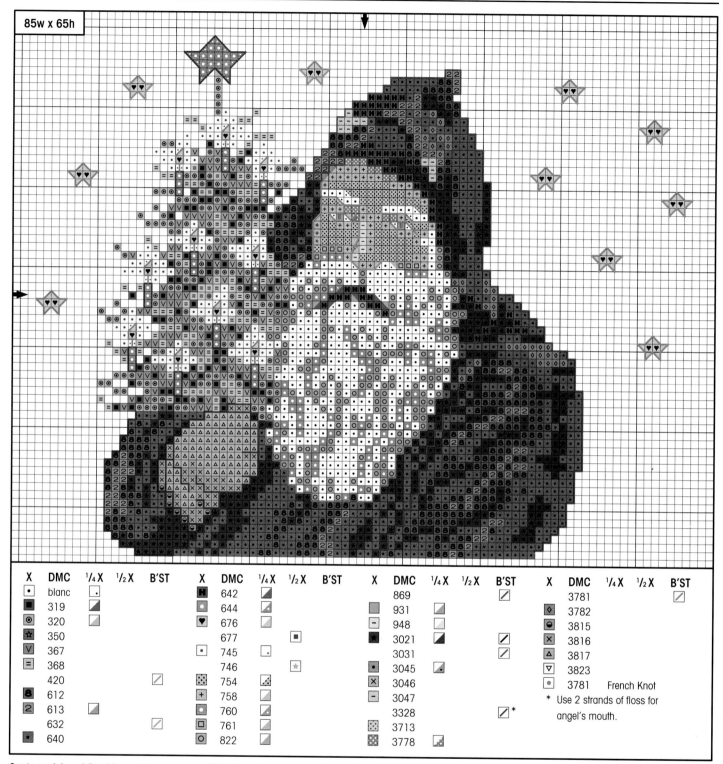

85w x 65h

| X | DMC | ¼ X | ½ X | B'ST | X | DMC | ¼ X | ½ X | B'ST | X | DMC | ¼ X | ½ X | B'ST | X | DMC | ¼ X | ½ X | B'ST |
|---|---|---|---|---|---|---|---|---|---|---|---|---|---|---|---|---|---|---|---|
| • | blanc | • | | | H | 642 | ◨ | | | | 869 | | | ◢ | ◆ | 3781 | | | ◢ |
| ■ | 319 | ◢ | | | ◙ | 644 | ◢ | | | | 931 | ◢ | | | ◆ | 3782 | | | |
| ◉ | 320 | ◢ | | | ♥ | 676 | ◢ | | | - | 948 | ◱ | | | ◐ | 3815 | | | |
| ✪ | 350 | | | | | 677 | | | ■ | ■ | 3021 | | | ◢ | ✕ | 3816 | | | |
| V | 367 | | | | • | 745 | • | | | | 3031 | | | ◢ | △ | 3817 | | | |
| = | 368 | | | | | 746 | | ★ | | • | 3045 | | ◢ | | ▽ | 3823 | | | |
| | 420 | | ◢ | ◌ | ◌ | 754 | ◢ | | | ✕ | 3046 | | | | • | 3781 | French Knot | | |
| 8 | 612 | | | + | + | 758 | ◢ | | | - | 3047 | | | | | | | | |
| 2 | 613 | | ◢ | ◉ | ◉ | 760 | ◢ | | | | 3328 | | | ◢ | * | * Use 2 strands of floss for | | |
| | 632 | | ◢ | □ | □ | 761 | ◢ | | | ◌ | 3713 | | | | | angel's mouth. | | |
| • | 640 | | | ○ | ○ | 822 | ◢ | | | ◌ | 3778 | | ◢ | | | | | | |

**Santa and Angel Stockings** (shown on page 14): Each design was stitched over 2 fabric threads on an 18" x 10" piece of Raw Belfast Linen (32 ct). Two strands of floss were used for Cross Stitch and 1 strand for Half Cross Stitch, Backstitch, and French Knots.

For each stocking, you will need a 15" x 7" piece of fabric for cuff backing, two 13" x 20" pieces of fabric for stocking, two 13" x 20" pieces of fabric for lining, 42" length of ½" dia. purchased cording with attached seam allowance, 2" x 5" piece of fabric for hanger, tracing paper, and fabric marking pencil.

Centering design, trim stitched piece to measure 15" x 7".

For stocking pattern, match arrows of Stocking Pattern, page 95, to form

one pattern and trace pattern onto tracing paper; add a ½" seam allowance on all sides and cut out pattern. Matching right sides and raw edges, place stocking fabric pieces together; place pattern on fabric pieces and pin pattern in place. Use fabric marking pencil to draw around pattern; remove pattern and cut out on drawn line. Repeat with lining fabric pieces.

If needed, trim seam allowance of cording to ½". Referring to photo for placement, match raw edges and baste cording to right side of one stocking piece. Matching right sides and leaving top open, use a ½" seam allowance to sew stocking pieces together. Clip seam allowance at curves and turn stocking right side out.

56

**86w x 66h**

*Needlework adaptations by Anne Stanton.*

Matching right sides and leaving top edge open, use a ⁵⁄₈" seam allowance to sew lining pieces together; trim seam allowance close to stitching. **Do not turn lining right side out.** With wrong sides facing, place lining inside stocking. Baste stocking and lining together close to raw edges.

For stocking cuff, match right sides and short edges; fold stitched piece in half. Using a ¹⁄₂" seam allowance, sew short edges together. Repeat for cuff backing. Matching right sides, raw edges, and seams, use a ¹⁄₂" seam allowance to sew cuff and cuff backing together along lower edge of cuff; turn right side out and press. Baste cuff and cuff backing together close to raw edges.

Referring to photo and matching raw edges, place right side of cuff to inside of stocking with cuff back seam at center back of stocking. Use a ¹⁄₂" seam allowance to sew cuff and stocking together. Fold cuff 4³⁄₄" to outside of stocking and press.

For hanger, press each long edge of fabric strip ¹⁄₂" to center. Matching long edges, fold strip in half and sew close to folded edges. Fold hanger in half, matching short edges; refer to photo and blind stitch to inside of stocking.

**Angel Hanging Pillow** (shown on page 19): The Angel design was stitched on a 12" x 11" piece of Parchment Hearthstone (14 ct). Three strands of floss were used for Cross Stitch and 1 strand for Half Cross Stitch, Backstitch, and French Knots.

For pillow, you will need a 12" x 11" piece of fabric for pillow backing, 26" length of ¹⁄₄" dia. purchased cord, two 18" lengths of ¹⁄₄" dia. purchased cord for hanger, and polyester fiberfill.

Matching right sides and raw edges, pin stitched piece and backing fabric together. Trim backing fabric and stitched piece ³⁄₄" larger than design on all sides. Leaving an opening for turning, use a ¹⁄₂" seam allowance to sew pieces together; trim seam allowance diagonally at corners. Turn pillow right side out, carefully pushing corners outward. Stuff pillow with polyester fiberfill and blind stitch opening closed. Beginning and ending at bottom center of pillow, blind stitch cord around edges of pillow.

For hanger, refer to photo and tack one length of cord to each upper corner of pillow back. Tie an overhand knot at ends and tie hanger in a bow.

## FINISHING INSTRUCTIONS

**Santa and Angels Afghan** (shown on page 19, chart on pages 54-55): For afghan, cut off selvages of fabric; measure 5¹⁄₂" from raw edge of fabric and pull out 1 fabric thread. Fringe fabric up to missing fabric thread. Repeat for each side. Tie an overhand knot at each corner with 4 horizontal and 4 vertical fabric threads. Working from corners, use 8 fabric threads for each knot until all threads are knotted.

**Diagram**

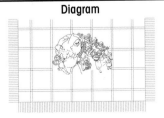

# LOVELY LIVING ROOM

| X | DMC | ¼X | B'ST | | X | DMC | ¼X | B'ST |
|---|-----|----|----|--|---|-----|----|----|
| • | blanc | • | | | ◓ | 931 | | |
| ▲ | 224 | ◢ | | | ◆ | 932 | | ◢ |
| ⊡* | 224 & | ◢ | | | ◇ | 950 | | ◢ |
| | 223 | | | | ∨ | 3045 | | ◢ |
| * | 225 | | | | ◓ | 3046 | | |
| | 317 | | ◢† | | • | 3047 | • | |
| ▣ | 318 | ◢ | | | ◨ | 3328 | ◢ | ◢† |
| | 347 | | ◢* | | ▲ | 3712 | | ◢ |
| 2 | 407 | ◢ | | | ≡ | 3713 | | |
| ☐ | 415 | ◢ | | | ◉ | 3752 | | |
| ◒ | 420 | ◢ | | | ♡ | 3753 | | ◢ |
| ◙ | 433 | ◢ | | | 2 | 3756 | | |
| ▨ | 434 | ◢ | ◢ | | ✕ | 3770 | | |
| ★ | 435 | ◢ | | | ▦ | 3773 | | ▨ |
| ◉ | 436 | ◢ | | | ▨ | 3774 | | ▨ |
| C | 437 | ◢ | | | * | 3820 | | ◢ |
| | 611 | | ◢ | | ☐ | 3821 | | |
| ▣ | 612 | ◢ | | | • | 3822 | • | |
| H | 613 | ◢ | | | − | 3823 | ⊡ | |
| | 632 | | ◢ | | | Kreinik | | ◢† |
| O | 644 | ◢ | | | | Cable - 002P | | |
| U | 738 | | | | ☐ | Blue area indicates first |
| ⊡ | 760 | ◢ | | | | row of right side of design. |
| ☆ | 761 | ◢ | | | * | Use 2 strands of first floss |
| + | 762 | ◢ | | | | color listed and 1 strand of |
| ▣ | 781 | ◢ | | | | second floss color listed. |
| ★ | 782 | ◢ | | | † | Use 3328 for mouths. |
| • | 783 | • | | | | Use Kreinik Cable for stars. |
| ♥ | 801 | ◢ | | | | Use 317 for all other. |
| ◎ | 819 | | | | * | Use 347 for pink gown. |
| ‖ | 822 | ◢ | | | | Use 930 for blue gown. |
| $ | 898 | | ◢ | | | |
| C | 930 | | ◢* | | | |

**Angels and Christ Child in Frame** (shown on page 15): The design was stitched over 2 fabric threads on a 19" square of Mushroom Lugana (25 ct). Three strands of floss were used for Cross Stitch and 1 strand of floss or cable for Backstitch. It was custom framed.

*Needlework adaptation by Donna Vermillion Giampa.*

STITCH COUNT (137w x 132h)

| | | | | |
|---|---|---|---|---|
| 14 count | 9⁷/₈" | x | 9¹/₂" |
| 16 count | 8⁵/₈" | x | 8¹/₄" |
| 18 count | 7⁵/₈" | x | 7³/₈" |
| 22 count | 6¹/₄" | x | 6" |

# Lovely Living Room

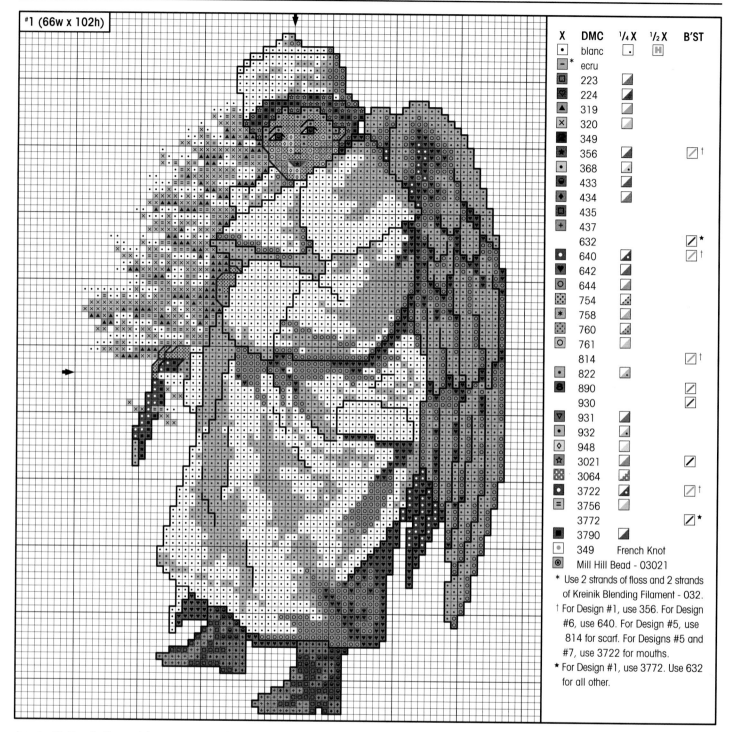

**#1 (66w x 102h)**

| X | DMC | ¼ X | ½ X | B'ST |
|---|---|---|---|---|
| • | blanc | • | H | |
| – * | ecru | | | |
| ▣ | 223 | ◪ | | |
| ▨ | 224 | ◪ | | |
| ▲ | 319 | ◪ | | |
| ✕ | 320 | ◪ | | |
| ■ | 349 | | | |
| ★ | 356 | ◪ | | ◪ † |
| • | 368 | • | | |
| ⬢ | 433 | ◪ | | |
| ◆ | 434 | ◪ | | |
| ▢ | 435 | | | |
| ✚ | 437 | | | |
| | 632 | | | ◪ * |
| ◨ | 640 | ◪ | | ◪ † |
| ♥ | 642 | ◪ | | |
| ◯ | 644 | ◪ | | |
| ▦ | 754 | ◪ | | |
| ✳ | 758 | ◪ | | |
| ▦ | 760 | ◪ | | |
| ◯ | 761 | | | |
| | 814 | | | ◪ † |
| • | 822 | • | | |
| ▨ | 890 | | | ◪ |
| | 930 | | | ◪ |
| ▽ | 931 | ◪ | | |
| • | 932 | • | | |
| ◇ | 948 | | | |
| ☆ | 3021 | ◪ | | ◪ |
| ▩ | 3064 | ◪ | | |
| ◉ | 3722 | ◪ | | ◪ † |
| = | 3756 | ◪ | | |
| | 3772 | | | ◪ * |
| ■ | 3790 | ◪ | | |
| ◉ | 349 | French Knot | | |
| ◎ | Mill Hill Bead - 03021 | | | |

\* Use 2 strands of floss and 2 strands of Kreinik Blending Filament - 032.

† For Design #1, use 356. For Design #6, use 640. For Design #5, use 814 for scarf. For Designs #5 and #7, use 3722 for mouths.

\* For Design #1, use 3772. Use 632 for all other.

**Angel with Tree in Frame** (shown on page 18): Design #1 was stitched over 2 fabric threads on a 13" x 16" piece of Mushroom Lugana (25 ct). Three strands of floss were used for Cross Stitch and 1 strand for Backstitch. It was custom framed.

*Needlework adaptation by Anne Stanton.*

**Snowflake Ornaments** (shown on pages 16-17): Designs #2, #3, and #4 were each stitched on a 5" square of Brown perforated paper (14 ct). Two strands of floss and 2 strands of blending filament were used for Cross Stitch. Attach beads using 2 strands of DMC ecru floss. See Attaching Beads, page 96.

Referring to photo, cut out stitched pieces close to designs.

**Snowflake Mitten Ornaments** (shown on pages 16-17): Designs #2, #3, and #4 were each stitched over 2 fabric threads on an 8" square of Raw Belfast Linen (32 ct). Two strands of floss and 2 strands of blending filament were used for Cross Stitch. Attach beads using 2 strands of DMC ecru floss. See Attaching Beads, page 96.

For each pair of mitten ornaments, you will need two of the same stitched design, two 8" square pieces of Belfast Linen for backing, tracing paper, pencil, fabric marking pencil, two 5½" lengths of ³⁄₈"w flat lace, and an 11" length of ¹⁄₈"w ribbon for hanger. To complete ornaments, see Finishing Instructions, page 95.

**Snowflake Coaster** (shown on page 15): Design #2 was stitched over 2 fabric threads on an 8" square of Raw Belfast Linen (32 ct). Two strands of floss and 2 strands of blending filament were used for Cross Stitch.

Centering design, trim stitched piece to 4¹⁄₂" square. Cross stitch border 1" from design on all sides using 2 strands of floss and 2 strands of blending filament. Fringe fabric, leaving 1 fabric thread between fringe and cross stitch border.

*Designs by Linda Culp Calhoun.*

**Angel Children and Santa Ornaments** (shown on pages 16-17): Designs #5, #6, and #7 were each stitched on an 8" x 10" piece of Parchment Hearthstone (14 ct). Three strands of floss were used for Cross Stitch and 1 strand for Half Cross Stitch, Backstitch, and French Knots.

For each ornament, you will need an 8" x 10" piece of Parchment Hearthstone for backing and polyester fiberfill.

Matching right sides and raw edges, pin stitched piece and backing fabric together. Leaving an opening for turning and stuffing, sew backing fabric to stitched piece ¹⁄₄" away from edge of design. Trim seam allowance to ¹⁄₄" and clip curves; turn right side out. Stuff ornament lightly with polyester fiberfill and blind stitch opening closed.

**Santa Shaker Box** (shown on page 18): Design #6 was stitched on an 8" x 10" piece of Parchment Hearthstone (14 ct). Three strands of floss were used for Cross Stitch and 1 strand for Backstitch.

For Shaker box, you will need a 4¹⁄₂" x 5³⁄₄" oval Shaker box, 4¹⁄₂" x 5³⁄₄" piece of batting for lid, 17¹⁄₂" length of ⁵⁄₈"w trim, tracing paper, pencil, and clear-drying craft glue.

For pattern, trace around box lid onto tracing paper; add ³⁄₄" on all sides and cut out. Referring to photo, position pattern on stitched piece and cut out. Clip ¹⁄₄" into edge of stitched piece at 1" intervals. Glue batting on top of lid and place wrong side of stitched piece on batting; fold edge of stitched piece down and glue to side of lid. Referring to photo, glue trim to side of lid.

*Needlework adaptations by Anne Stanton.*

# delightful dining

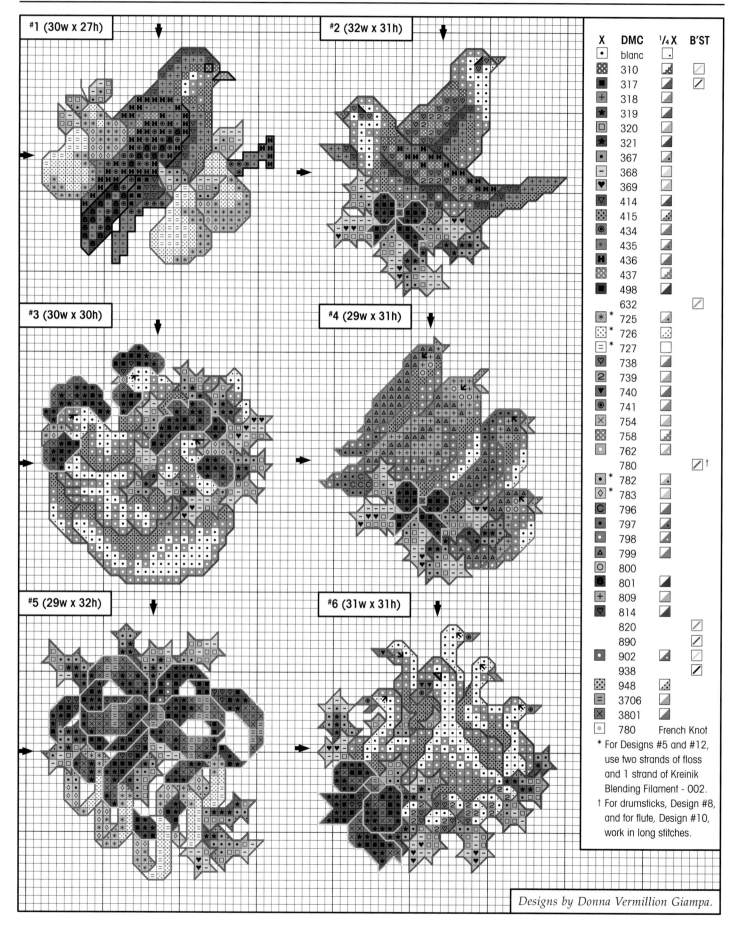

#1 (30w x 27h)  
#2 (32w x 31h)  
#3 (30w x 30h)  
#4 (29w x 31h)  
#5 (29w x 32h)  
#6 (31w x 31h)

| X | DMC | ¼ X | B'ST |
|---|---|---|---|
| • | blanc | | |
| | 310 | | |
| | 317 | | |
| | 318 | | |
| | 319 | | |
| | 320 | | |
| | 321 | | |
| • | 367 | | |
| – | 368 | | |
| ♥ | 369 | | |
| ▽ | 414 | | |
| | 415 | | |
| ◉ | 434 | | |
| • | 435 | | |
| H | 436 | | |
| | 437 | | |
| | 498 | | |
| | 632 | | |
| ✳ * | 725 | | |
| | 726 | | |
| ═ * | 727 | | |
| ▽ | 738 | | |
| 2 | 739 | | |
| ▼ | 740 | | |
| ◉ | 741 | | |
| ✕ | 754 | | |
| | 758 | | |
| | 762 | | |
| | 780 | | |
| • * | 782 | | |
| ◇ * | 783 | | |
| C | 796 | | |
| • | 797 | | |
| • | 798 | | |
| ▲ | 799 | | |
| O | 800 | | |
| | 801 | | |
| + | 809 | | |
| ♥ | 814 | | |
| | 820 | | |
| | 890 | | |
| • | 902 | | |
| | 938 | | |
| | 948 | | |
| ═ | 3706 | | |
| ✕ | 3801 | | |
| • | 780 | French Knot | |

* For Designs #5 and #12, use two strands of floss and 1 strand of Kreinik Blending Filament - 002.

† For drumsticks, Design #8, and for flute, Design #10, work in long stitches.

*Designs by Donna Vermillion Giampa.*

62

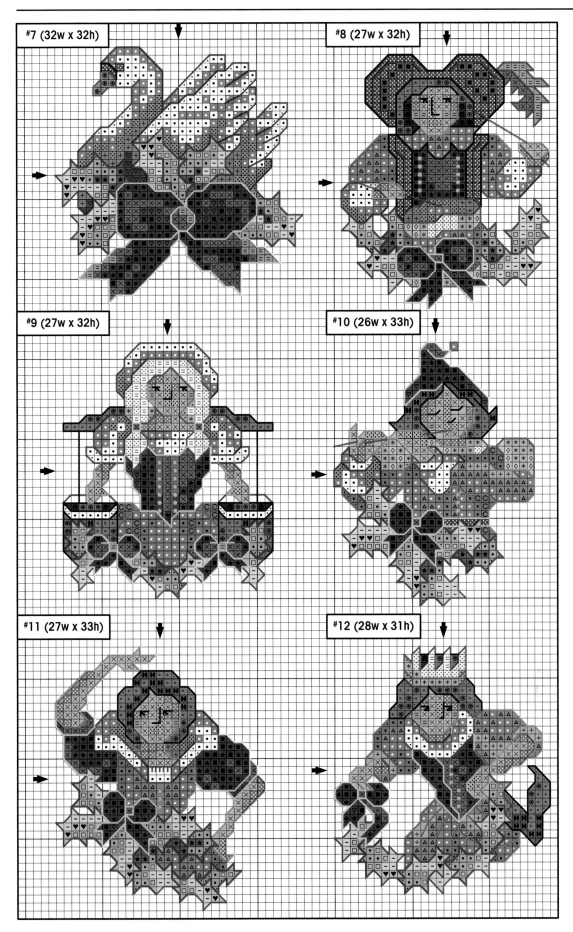

#7 (32w x 32h)

#8 (27w x 32h)

#9 (27w x 32h)

#10 (26w x 33h)

#11 (27w x 33h)

#12 (28w x 31h)

**Twelve Days of Christmas Ornaments** (shown on pages 22-23): Each design was stitched on a 4" square of Dirty Aida (18 ct). Two strands of floss were used for Cross Stitch and 1 strand for Backstitch and French Knots, unless otherwise noted in the color key. They were inserted in purchased gold round frames (2¹/₂" dia. opening).

**Twelve Days of Christmas Napkins** (shown on page 24): Designs #6, #10, and #11 were each stitched over a 5" square of 11 mesh waste canvas in one corner of a purchased napkin. Four strands of floss were used for Cross Stitch and 2 strands for Backstitch. Refer to photo for placement of design.

**Working on Waste Canvas:** Waste canvas is a special canvas that provides an evenweave grid for placing stitches on fabric. After the design is worked over the canvas, the canvas threads are removed, leaving the design on the fabric. The canvas is available in several mesh sizes.

Cover edges of canvas with masking tape. For napkins only, cut a piece of lightweight non-fusible interfacing the same size as canvas to provide a firm stitching base.

Find desired stitching area and mark center of area with a pin. Match center of canvas to pin. Use the blue threads in canvas to place canvas straight on project; pin canvas to project. For napkins only, pin interfacing to wrong side of project. Baste all layers together.

Using a sharp needle, work design, stitching from large holes to large holes. Trim canvas to within ³/₄" of design. Dampen canvas until it becomes limp. Pull out canvas threads one at a time using tweezers. For napkins only, trim interfacing close to design.

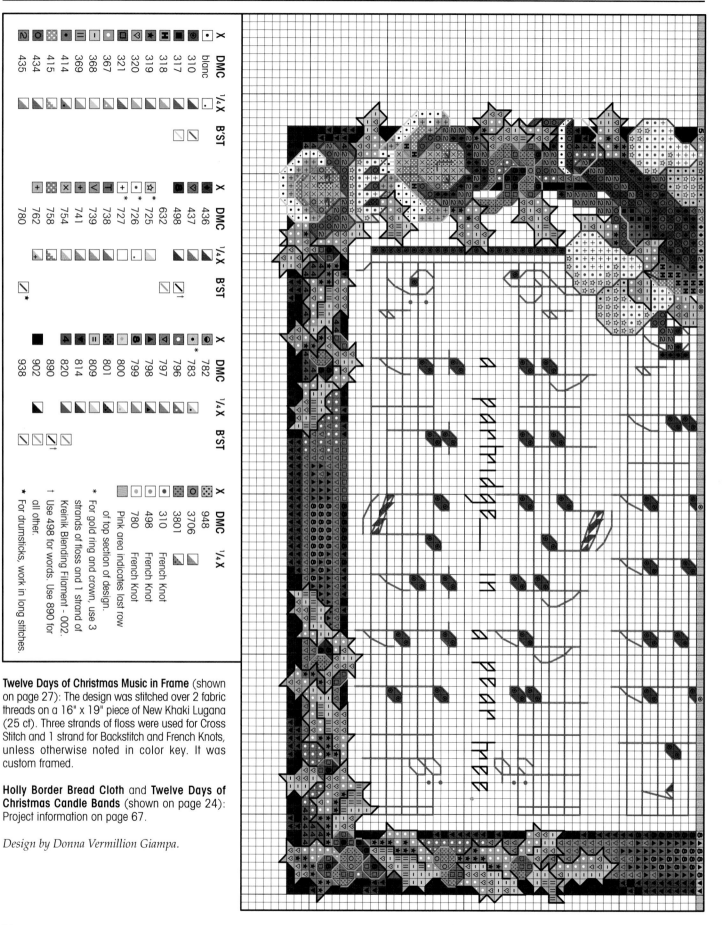

Color Key:

| X | ¼X | B'ST | DMC |
|---|---|---|---|
|  |  |  | blanc |
|  |  |  | 310 |
|  |  |  | 317 |
|  |  |  | 318 |
|  |  |  | 319 |
|  |  |  | 320 |
|  |  |  | 321 |
|  |  |  | 367 |
|  |  |  | 368 |
|  |  |  | 369 |
|  |  |  | 414 |
|  |  |  | 415 |
|  |  |  | 434 |
|  |  |  | 435 |

| X | ¼X | B'ST | DMC |
|---|---|---|---|
|  |  |  | 436 |
|  |  |  | 437 |
|  |  |  | 498 |
|  |  |  | 632 |
|  |  |  | 725 |
|  |  |  | 726 |
|  |  |  | 727 |
|  |  |  | 738 |
|  |  |  | 739 |
|  |  |  | 741 |
|  |  |  | 754 |
|  |  |  | 758 |
|  |  |  | 762 |
|  |  |  | 780 |

| X | ¼X | B'ST | DMC |
|---|---|---|---|
|  |  |  | 782 |
|  |  |  | 783 |
|  |  |  | 796 |
|  |  |  | 797 |
|  |  |  | 798 |
|  |  |  | 799 |
|  |  |  | 800 |
|  |  |  | 801 |
|  |  |  | 809 |
|  |  |  | 814 |
|  |  |  | 820 |
|  |  |  | 890 |
|  |  |  | 902 |
|  |  |  | 938 |

| X | ¼X | DMC |
|---|---|---|
|  |  | 948 |
|  |  | 3706 |
|  |  | 3801 |
|  |  | 310 French Knot |
|  |  | 498 French Knot |
|  |  | 780 French Knot |

Pink area indicates last row of top section of design.

\* For gold ring and crown, use 3 strands of floss and 1 strand of Kreinik Blending Filament - 002.

† Use 498 for words. Use 890 for all other.

★ For drumsticks, work in long stitches.

**Twelve Days of Christmas Music in Frame** (shown on page 27): The design was stitched over 2 fabric threads on a 16" x 19" piece of New Khaki Lugana (25 ct). Three strands of floss were used for Cross Stitch and 1 strand for Backstitch and French Knots, unless otherwise noted in color key. It was custom framed.

**Holly Border Bread Cloth** and **Twelve Days of Christmas Candle Bands** (shown on page 24): Project information on page 67.

*Design by Donna Vermillion Giampa.*

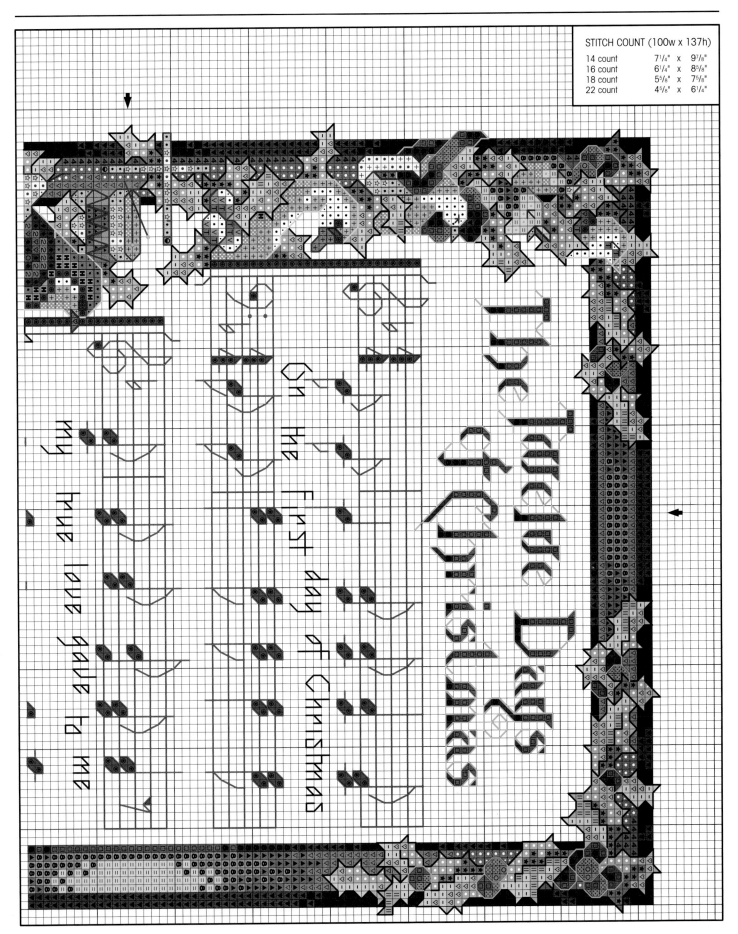

STITCH COUNT (100w x 137h)

| 14 count | 7¼" | x | 9⅞" |
| 16 count | 6¼" | x | 8⅝" |
| 18 count | 5⅝" | x | 7⅝" |
| 22 count | 4⅝" | x | 6¼" |

# delightful dining

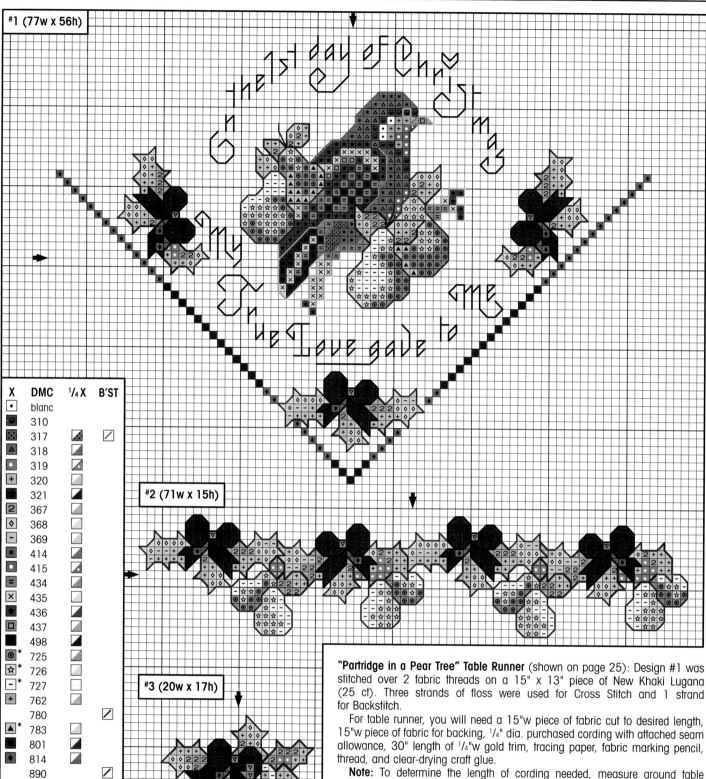

#1 (77w x 56h)

On the 1st day of Christmas my true Love gave to me

#2 (71w x 15h)

#3 (20w x 17h)

| X | DMC | 1/4 X | B'ST |
|---|---|---|---|
| • | blanc | | |
| ■ | 310 | | |
| ▨ | 317 | ◺ | ◿ |
| ▲ | 318 | ◺ | |
| ◉ | 319 | ◺ | |
| + | 320 | ◺ | |
| ■ | 321 | ◺ | |
| 2 | 367 | ◺ | |
| ◈ | 368 | ◺ | |
| − | 369 | ◺ | |
| ✳ | 414 | ◺ | |
| ▣ | 415 | ◺ | |
| ▦ | 434 | ◺ | |
| × | 435 | ◺ | |
| ★ | 436 | ◺ | |
| □ | 437 | ◺ | |
| ■ | 498 | ◺ | |
| ◉ | 725* | ◺ | |
| ☆ | 726* | ◺ | |
| − | 727* | □ | |
| + | 762 | ◺ | |
| | 780 | | ◿ |
| ▲ | 783* | ◺ | |
| ■ | 801 | ◺ | |
| ◆ | 814 | ◺ | |
| | 890 | | ◿ |
| | 902 | | ◿ |
| | 938 | | ◿ |
| ▽ | 3801 | ◺ | |

* For Design #3, use
3 strands of floss
and 1 strand of
Kreinik Blending
Filament - 002.

"Partridge in a Pear Tree" Table Runner (shown on page 25): Design #1 was stitched over 2 fabric threads on a 15" x 13" piece of New Khaki Lugana (25 ct). Three strands of floss were used for Cross Stitch and 1 strand for Backstitch.

For table runner, you will need a 15"w piece of fabric cut to desired length, 15"w piece of fabric for backing, 1/4" dia. purchased cording with attached seam allowance, 30" length of 1/4"w gold trim, tracing paper, fabric marking pencil, thread, and clear-drying craft glue.

**Note:** To determine the length of cording needed, measure around table runner and add 4". Use a 1/2" seam allowance for all seams.

Matching right sides and raw edges, place table runner fabric and backing fabric pieces together. Referring to **Fig. 1**, use a fabric marking pencil to draw points on each short edge of fabric pieces. Cut along drawn lines.

If needed, trim seam allowance of cording to 1/2". Beginning 2" from end of cording and in the middle of one long edge of table runner front, pin cording to right side of table runner front. Make 3/8" clips in seam allowance of cording at points. Ends of cording should overlap approximately 4". Turn overlapped ends of cording toward outside edge of table runner front; baste cording to table runner front.

Matching right sides and raw edges and leaving an opening for turning, sew table runner front to table runner back. Trim seam allowances and clip corners; turn right side out, carefully pushing corners outward. Blind stitch opening closed.

For pattern to trim stitched piece, fold tracing paper in half and place fold on dashed line of pattern; trace pattern onto tracing paper. Cut out pattern; unfold and press flat.

Referring to photo, position pattern on wrong side of stitched piece; pin pattern in place. Use a fabric marking pencil to draw around pattern; remove pattern and cut out on drawn line.

Referring to photo for placement, position stitched piece at one end of table runner with raw edges 1" away from edges of point. Attach stitched piece to table runner using a zigzag stitch. Glue gold trim around stitched piece, covering raw edges.

**Fig. 1**

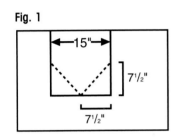

**Pear Border Wine Bag** (shown on page 20): Design #2 was stitched over 2 fabric threads on an 18" x 7" piece of New Khaki Lugana (25 ct). Three strands of floss were used for Cross Stitch and 1 strand for Backstitch.

For wine bag, you will need a 6½" x 32" piece of fabric, ¼"w gold trim, coordinating ribbon, assorted greenery, a jingle bell, and fabric glue.

**Note:** We used a bottle measuring 10" around x 11½" high. If using a different size bottle, fabric and stitched piece measurements may need to be adjusted. To determine the measurement of fabric needed, measure around bottle; divide measurement by 2 and add 1½". Measure bottle from one side of top to opposite side of top (**Fig. 2**); add 6". Cut a piece of fabric the determined measurements.

**Fig. 2**

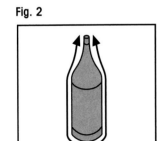

Matching right sides and short edges, fold fabric in half; finger press folded edge (bottom of bag). Using a ¼" seam allowance, sew sides of bag together.

For boxed corners, match each side seam to fold line at bottom of bag; sew across each corner 1" from point (**Fig. 3**).

**Fig. 3**

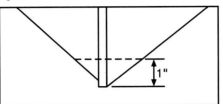

Press top edge of bag ¼" to wrong side; press ½" to wrong side again and stitch in place. Turn bag right side out.

Centering design, trim stitched piece to measure 3" x 14".

Turn each short end 1" to wrong side of stitched piece; whipstitch in place. With design centered on front of bag and top edge of stitched piece 8" from top edge of bag, whipstitch long edges of stitched piece to bag. Whipstitch short edges together. Referring to photo, glue gold trim to stitched piece, covering raw edges.

Place bottle in bag. Tie ribbon into a bow around top of bag. Referring to photo, attach bell and greenery to bow.

**"Five Golden Rings" Cracker** (shown on page 25): Design #3 was stitched over 2 fabric threads on an 8" square of New Khaki Lugana (25 ct). Three strands of floss were used for Cross Stitch and 1 strand for Backstitch, unless otherwise noted in the color key.

For cracker, you will need a 7½" x 14" piece of coordinating fabric, one 5" length of 1½" dia. cardboard tube, two 14" lengths of ⅛"w black ribbon, and clear-drying craft glue.

Fold each long edge of fabric ½" to wrong side; glue in place. Fold each short edge 2" to wrong side; glue in place. Insert candy or small gift in tube and center tube lengthwise on wrong side of fabric. Fold long edges of fabric around tube; glue overlapping edges of fabric along length of tube only. Tie fabric with one length of ribbon at each end of tube.

With design centered, trim stitched piece to measure 6½" x 7". Matching right sides and long edges, fold stitched piece in half. Use ¼" seam allowance to sew long edges together. Trim seam allowance to ⅛" and turn stitched piece right side out. With seam centered in back, press stitched piece flat. Press short edges ½" to wrong side.

Center and wrap stitched piece around cracker; blind stitch short edges together.

**Holly Border Bread Cloth** (shown on page 24, chart on page 64): The holly design in the bottom right corner of the Twelve Days of Christmas Music (refer to photo, page 24) was stitched over 2 fabric threads in one corner of an 18" square of New Khaki Lugana (25 ct) with design 1½" from raw edges of fabric. Three strands of floss were used for Cross Stitch and 1 strand for Backstitch.

For bread cloth, machine stitch around fabric ½" from raw edges. Fringe to machine-stitched line.

**Twelve Days of Christmas Candle Bands** (shown on page 24, chart on pages 64-65): The first and second lines of the Twelve Days of Christmas Music (refer to photo, page 24) were each stitched over 2 fabric threads on an 18" x 8" piece of New Khaki Lugana (25 ct). Three strands of floss were used for Cross Stitch and 1 strand for Backstitch and French Knots.

For each candle band, you will need an 18" x 4" piece of fabric for backing, two 18" lengths of ¼"w gold trim, and fabric glue.

Centering design, trim stitched piece to measure 18" x 4".

Matching wrong sides and long edges, use a ¼" seam allowance to sew long edges of stitched piece and backing fabric together. Referring to photo, glue gold trim to long edges of stitched piece. Wrap candle band around candle, turning raw edges to wrong side so that ends meet; blind stitch short ends together.

*Designs by Donna Vermillion Giampa.*

# FESTIVE FAMILY ROOM

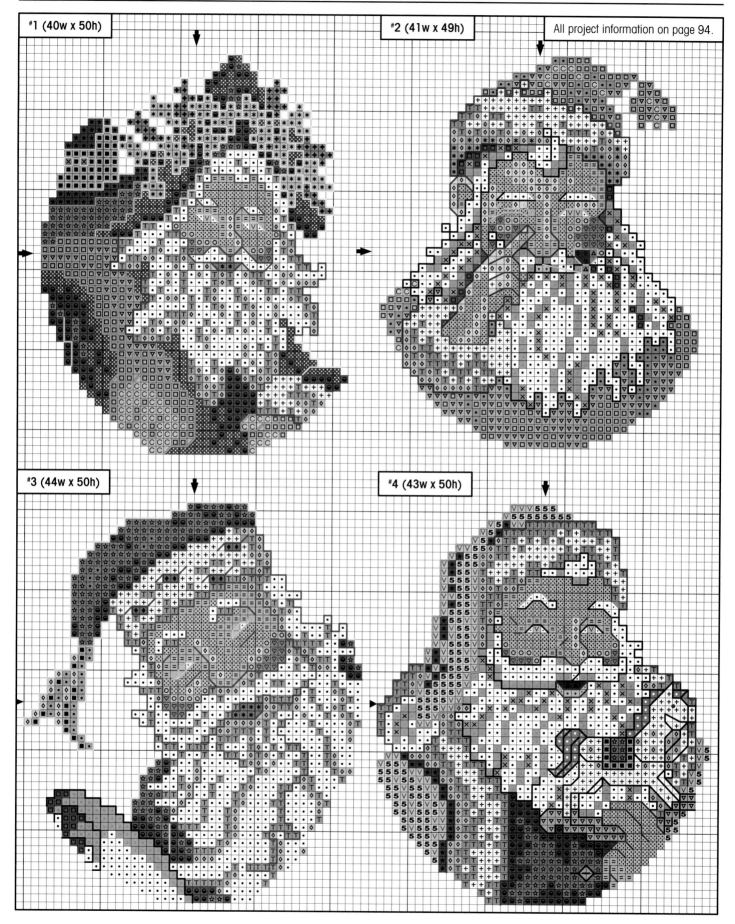

#1 (40w x 50h)

#2 (41w x 49h)

All project information on page 94.

#3 (44w x 50h)

#4 (43w x 50h)

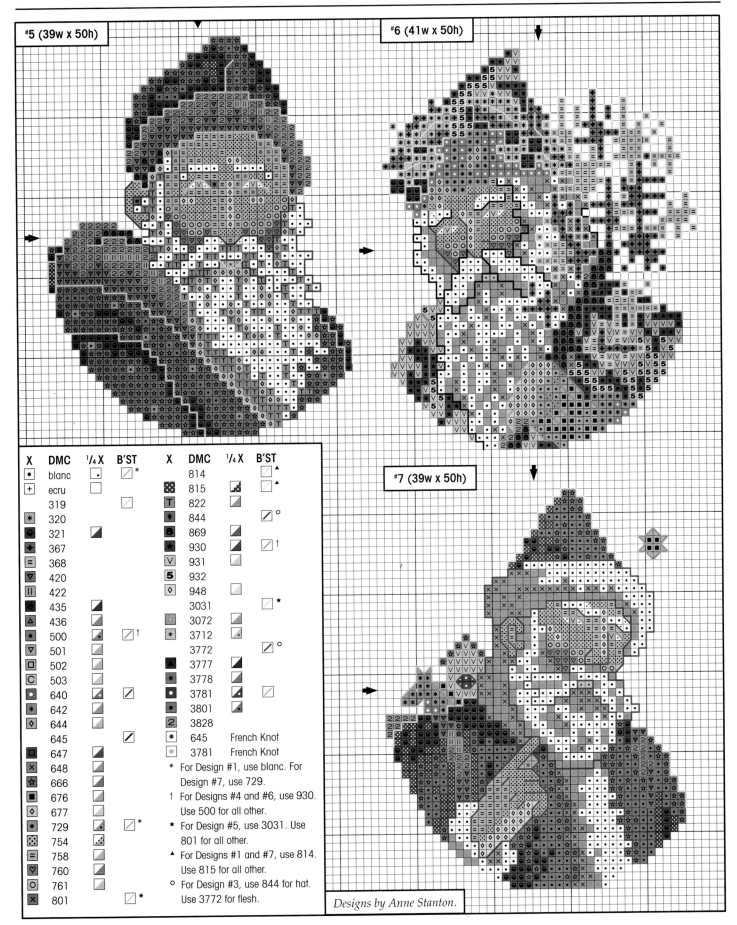

#5 (39w x 50h)

#6 (41w x 50h)

#7 (39w x 50h)

| X | DMC | 1/4 X | B'ST | X | DMC | 1/4 X | B'ST |
|---|---|---|---|---|---|---|---|
| • | blanc | • | / * | | 814 | | ◣ |
| + | ecru | □ | | ▦ | 815 | | ◣ |
| | 319 | | / | T | 822 | | ◣ |
| * | 320 | | | ◆ | 844 | | / ° |
| ● | 321 | ◣ | | ● | 869 | | ◣ |
| ✦ | 367 | | | ★ | 930 | | ◣ † |
| = | 368 | | | V | 931 | ◣ | |
| ▽ | 420 | | | 5 | 932 | ◣ | |
| ‖ | 422 | | | ◇ | 948 | ◣ | |
| ◩ | 435 | ◣ | | | 3031 | | / ★ |
| ▲ | 436 | ◣ | | ▪ | 3072 | | |
| • | 500 | ◣ | / † | • | 3712 | | • |
| ▽ | 501 | ◣ | | | 3772 | | / ° |
| □ | 502 | ◣ | | ■ | 3777 | ◣ | |
| C | 503 | ◣ | | * | 3778 | ◣ | |
| ◪ | 640 | ◣ | / | ◉ | 3781 | ◣ | / |
| * | 642 | ◣ | | ● | 3801 | ◣ | |
| ◇ | 644 | ◣ | | 2 | 3828 | | |
| | 645 | | / | • | 645 | French Knot | |
| ■ | 647 | ◣ | | ○ | 3781 | French Knot | |
| ✕ | 648 | ◣ | | | | | |
| ☆ | 666 | ◣ | | | | | |
| ■ | 676 | ◣ | | | | | |
| ◇ | 677 | ◣ | | | | | |
| • | 729 | ◣ | / * | | | | |
| ▦ | 754 | ◣ | | | | | |
| = | 758 | ◣ | | | | | |
| ▽ | 760 | ◣ | | | | | |
| ○ | 761 | ◣ | | | | | |
| ✕ | 801 | | / * | | | | |

* For Design #1, use blanc. For Design #7, use 729.

† For Designs #4 and #6, use 930. Use 500 for all other.

★ For Design #5, use 3031. Use 801 for all other.

▲ For Designs #1 and #7, use 814. Use 815 for all other.

° For Design #3, use 844 for hat. Use 3772 for flesh.

*Designs by Anne Stanton.*

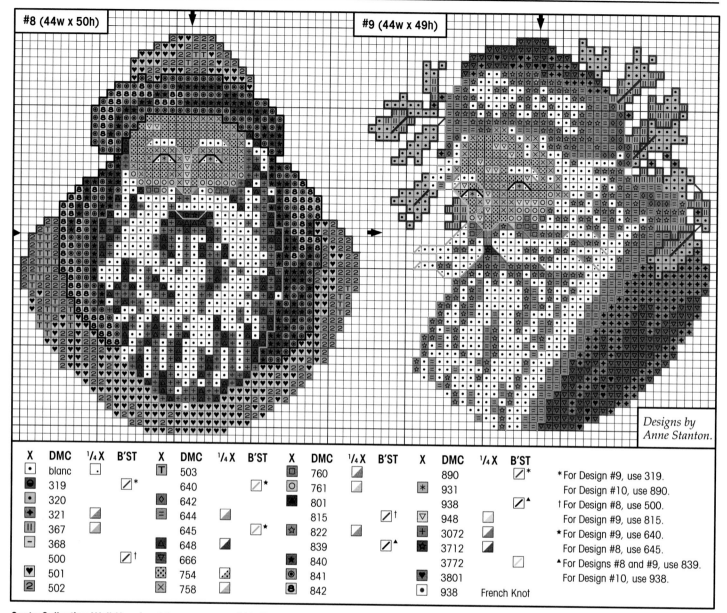

#8 (44w x 50h)  #9 (44w x 49h)

*Designs by Anne Stanton.*

| X | DMC | ¼X | B'ST | X | DMC | ¼X | B'ST | X | DMC | ¼X | B'ST | X | DMC | ¼X | B'ST | |
|---|---|---|---|---|---|---|---|---|---|---|---|---|---|---|---|---|
| • | blanc | • | | T | 503 | | | ▢ | 760 | | ◸ | | 890 | | ◸* | *For Design #9, use 319. |
| ◉ | 319 | | ◸* | | 640 | | ◸* | ○ | 761 | | ◸ | * | 931 | | | For Design #10, use 890. |
| ⊡ | 320 | | | ◈ | 642 | | | ▪ | 801 | | | | 938 | | ◸▲ | †For Design #8, use 500. |
| ✦ | 321 | ◺ | | ≡ | 644 | ◺ | | | 815 | | ◸† | ▽ | 948 | ◺ | | For Design #9, use 815. |
| ‖ | 367 | ◺ | | | 645 | | ◸* | ☆ | 822 | ◺ | | + | 3072 | ◺ | | *For Design #9, use 640. |
| – | 368 | | | ▲ | 648 | ◺ | | | 839 | | ◸▲ | ▧ | 3712 | ◺ | | For Design #8, use 645. |
| | 500 | | ◸† | ▽ | 666 | | | ★ | 840 | | | | 3772 | | | ▲For Designs #8 and #9, use 839. |
| ♥ | 501 | | | ▨ | 754 | ⣿ | | ◉ | 841 | | | ♥ | 3801 | | ◸ | For Design #10, use 938. |
| 2 | 502 | | | ✕ | 758 | ◺ | | 8 | 842 | | | • | 938 | | French Knot | |

**Santa Collection Wall Hanging** (shown on page 31): Each design was stitched over 2 fabric threads on an 8" square of Cream Cashel Linen® (28 ct). Three strands of floss were used for Cross Stitch and 1 strand for Backstitch and French Knots.

For wall hanging, you will need 60"w wool fabric (¼ yd of green and ⅔ yd of red plaid), batting, thread, and 16 assorted buttons.

Centering design, trim each stitched piece to measure 5½" square.

Referring to tables below, cut the number of pieces specified from the fabrics indicated.

**Note:** When piecing wall hanging, always match right sides and raw edges. Use a ½" seam allowance for all seams.

Referring to Diagram for placement, join stitched pieces and A fabric pieces to form three vertical rows. Referring to Diagram, sew vertical rows to B fabric pieces. Working in alphabetical order, sew border fabric pieces to wall hanging.

| GREEN FABRIC | | |
|---|---|---|
| FABRIC PIECE | QUANTITY | SIZE |
| A | 6 | 2" x 5½" |
| B | 2 | 2" x 16½" |
| C | 2 | 2" x 16½" |
| D | 2 | 2" x 18½" |

| RED PLAID FABRIC | | |
|---|---|---|
| FABRIC PIECE | QUANTITY | SIZE |
| E | 2 | 3" x 18½" |
| F | 2 | 3" x 22½" |

**DIAGRAM**

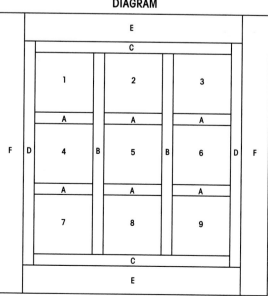

Continued on page 94.

**#10 (83w X 83h)**

*I will honor Christmas in my heart and try to keep it all year. Charles Dickens*

**"I Will Honor Christmas" in Frame** (shown on page 35): Design #10 was stitched over 2 fabric threads on a 14" square of Cream Cashel Linen® (28 ct). Three strands of floss were used for Cross Stitch and 1 strand for Backstitch and French Knots. It was custom framed.

**"I Will Honor Christmas" Pillow** (shown on page 28): Design #10 was stitched over 2 fabric threads on a 14" square of Cream Cashel Linen® (28 ct). Three strands of floss were used for Cross Stitch and 1 strand for Backstitch and French Knots.

For pillow, you will need a 13½" square piece of red plaid fabric for backing, two 2" x 7½" strips of green fabric for top and bottom borders, two 2" x 9½" strips of green fabric for side borders, two 3" x 10½" strips of red plaid fabric for outer top and bottom borders, two 3" x 13½" strips of red plaid fabric for outer side borders, thread, polyester fiberfill, and four 1" dia. red buttons.

Centering design, trim stitched piece to measure 7½" square.

**Note:** When piecing pillow, always match right sides and raw edges. Use a ½" seam allowance for all seams.

For pillow front, sew top green border strip to top edge of stitched piece. Repeat with bottom green border strip and bottom edge of stitched piece. Press seam allowances toward strips. Sew one side green border strip to one side edge of stitched piece and top and bottom strips. Repeat with remaining side green border strip and side edge. Press seam allowances toward strips. For outer border, repeat with red plaid top, bottom, and side border strips. Referring to photo, sew buttons to pillow front.

Matching right sides and leaving an opening for turning, sew pillow front and backing fabric together. Trim seam allowances diagonally at corners; turn pillow right side out, carefully pushing corners outward. Stuff pillow with polyester fiberfill and blind stitch opening closed.

*Design by Deborah Lambein.*

71

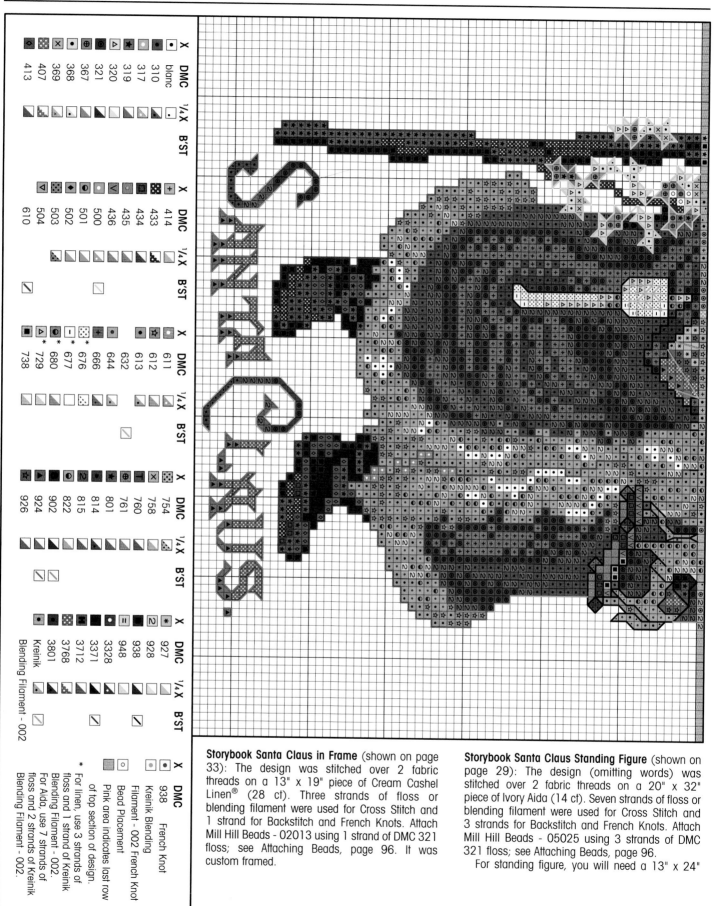

**Storybook Santa Claus in Frame** (shown on page 33): The design was stitched over 2 fabric threads on a 13" x 19" piece of Cream Cashel Linen® (28 ct). Three strands of floss or blending filament were used for Cross Stitch and 1 strand for Backstitch and French Knots. Attach Mill Hill Beads - 02013 using 1 strand of DMC 321 floss; see Attaching Beads, page 96. It was custom framed.

**Storybook Santa Claus Standing Figure** (shown on page 29): The design (omitting words) was stitched over 2 fabric threads on a 20" x 32" piece of Ivory Aida (14 ct). Seven strands of floss or blending filament were used for Cross Stitch and 3 strands for Backstitch and French Knots. Attach Mill Hill Beads - 05025 using 3 strands of DMC 321 floss; see Attaching Beads, page 96.

For standing figure, you will need a 13" x 24"

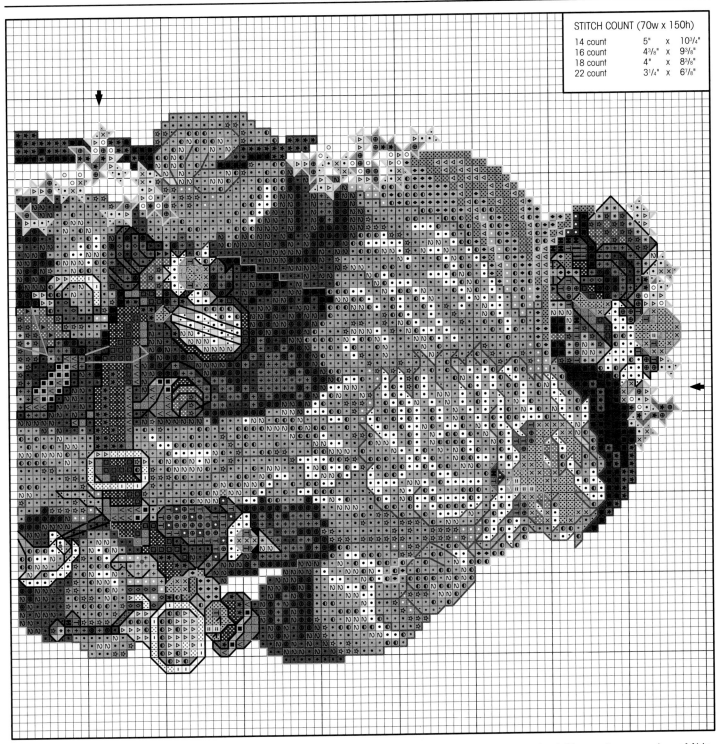

STITCH COUNT (70w x 150h)

| | | | |
|---|---|---|---|
| 14 count | 5" | x | 10³/₄" |
| 16 count | 4³/₈" | x | 9³/₈" |
| 18 count | 4" | x | 8³/₈" |
| 22 count | 3¹/₄" | x | 6⁷/₈" |

piece of Aida for backing, a 9" x 8" piece of Aida for base, tracing paper, fabric marking pencil, small plastic bag, aquarium gravel, and polyester fiberfill.

Centering design, trim stitched piece to measure 13" x 24".

Matching right sides and raw edges and leaving bottom edge open, sew stitched piece and backing together ¹/₈" from design. Trim bottom edge of figure ³/₄" from bottom of design. Leaving a ¹/₄" seam allowance, cut out figure. Clip seam allowances at curves; turn figure right side out and carefully push curves outward. Press raw edges at bottom ¹/₄" to wrong side; stuff figure with polyester fiberfill to 1¹/₂" from opening.

For base, place figure on tracing paper and draw around figure. Add

a ¹/₂" seam allowance to pattern; cut out. Place pattern on a piece of Aida. Use fabric marking pencil to draw around pattern; cut out along drawn line. Baste around base piece ¹/₂" from raw edge; press raw edges to wrong side along basting line.

To weight bottom of figure, fill a plastic bag with a small amount of aquarium gravel. Insert bag of gravel into opening of figure.

Pin wrong side of base piece over opening. Whipstitch in place, adding polyester fiberfill as necessary to fill bottom of figure. Remove basting thread.

*Needlework adaptation by Donna Vermillion Giampa.*

# festive family room

| X | DMC | B'ST |
|---|---|---|
| ▣ | 310 | ✓ |
| ◎ | 317 | |
| − | 318 | |
| 2 | 319 | |
| ＊ | 320 | |
| ◩ | 321 | |
| ♥ | 367 | |
| = | 368 | |
| ▽ | 369 | |
| ◇ | 676 | |
| ♡ | 677 | |
| ■ | 729 | |
| ☆ | 746 | |
| ✕ | 801 | |
| | 938 | ✓ |
| ▣ | 3799 | |
| | Kreinik | ✓ |
| | Fine Braid - 002 | |

65w x 98h

46w x 92h

**"O Christmas Tree" and "Joy to All" Stockings** (shown on page 32): Each design was stitched over 2 fabric threads on a 13" x 16" piece of Cream Lugana (25 ct) with top of design 3" from one short edge of fabric. Three strands of floss were used for Cross Stitch and 1 strand of floss or 2 strands of braid for Backstitch.

For each stocking, you will need a 13" x 16" piece of Cream Lugana for backing, two 7" x 12" pieces of fabric for lining, 9½" x 5" piece of fabric for cuff, 6" x 2" piece of fabric for hanger, tracing paper, fabric marking pencil, and assorted buttons.

Match arrows of Stocking Pattern, page 94, to form one pattern and trace pattern onto tracing paper; add ½" seam allowance on all sides and cut out pattern. Referring to photo for placement, position pattern on wrong side of stitched piece; pin pattern in place. Use fabric marking pencil to draw around pattern; remove pattern and cut out on drawn line. Use pattern and cut **one** from backing fabric and **two** from lining fabric.

Matching right sides and leaving top edge open, use a ½" seam allowance to sew stitched piece and backing fabric together; clip seam allowance at

curves and turn stocking right side out.

Matching right sides and leaving top edge open, use a ⅝" seam allowance to sew lining fabric together; trim seam allowance close to stitching. **Do not turn lining right side out.** With wrong sides facing, place lining inside stocking; baste lining and stocking together close to top edge.

Matching right sides and short edges of cuff fabric, use a ½" seam allowance to sew short edges together. Matching wrong sides and raw edges, fold cuff in half and press. Matching raw edges, place cuff inside stocking with cuff seam at center back of stocking. Use ½" seam allowance to sew cuff, stocking, and lining together. Fold cuff 2" over stocking and press.

For hanger, press each long edge of fabric strip ½" to center. Fold strip in half, matching long edges; sew close to folded edges. Matching short edges, fold hanger in half and blind stitch to inside of stocking at right seam.

Referring to photo, sew assorted buttons to stockings.

*Designs by Deborah Lambein.*

# home sweet holiday

**64w x 94h**

| X | DMC | 1/4 X | B'ST |
|---|---|---|---|
| • | blanc | • | |
| 2 | 321 | ◢ | ◢ * |
| ▼ | 407 | ◢ | |
| ◖ | 433 | ◢ | |
| ▽ | 434 | | |
| T | 435 | | |
| ◙ | 436 | ◢ | |
| ✳ | 437 | ◢ | ◢ * |
| | 632 | ◢ | ◢ * |
| O | 666 | | |
| ◎ | 725 | ☐ | |
| • | 727 | • | |
| ♡ | 738 | | |
| ‖ | 739 | | |
| ▨ | 754 | ◢ | |
| ✕ | 758 | ◢ | |
| H | 760 | ◢ | |
| = † | 760 & | | ◢ |
| | 761 | | |
| ▨ | 762 | ◢ | |
| | 780 | | ◢ * |
| + | 782 | | |
| ◇ | 783 | ◢ | |
| ■ | 814 | ◢ | |
| ✿ | 815 | ◢ | |
| | 838 | | ◢ * |
| | 898 | | ◢ * ▲ |
| ★ | 902 | ◢ | |
| ◆ | 924 | ◢ | ◢ |
| ▨ | 926 | ◢ | |
| ▨ † | 927 & | ◢ | |
| | 3024 | | |
| − | 928 | ◢ | |
| ♥ | 935 | ◢ | ◢ |
| ◇ | 948 | ◢ | |
| • | 3021 | ◢ | ◢ |
| ☐ | 3022 | ◢ | |
| ▨ | 3023 | ◢ | |
| △ | 3024 | ◢ | |
| ▨ | 3328 | ◢ | |
| ◆ | 3362 | ◢ | |
| ☐ | 3363 | ◢ | |
| U | 3364 | | |
| ▢ | 3768 | ◢ | |
| ▨ | 3773 | ◢ | |
| ✳ | 3787 | ◢ | ◢ |
| + | 3801 | | |
| ◉ | 632 | French Knot | |

* Use 321 for drum and
  package. Use 632 for
  all other.
† Use one strand of each
  floss color listed.
★ Use 780 for doll and stars.
  Use 898 for switches. Use
  838 for all other.
▲ Work in long stitches.

**Christmas Visitor Wreath** (shown on page 6): The design was stitched over 2 fabric threads on a 12" x 14" piece of Antique White Belfast Linen (32 ct). Two strands of floss were used for Cross Stitch and 1 strand for Backstitch and French Knots. It was inserted in a purchased frame (5" x 7" opening) and attached to a decorated 18" dia. wreath.

*Needlework adaptation by Donna Vermillion Giampa.*

# home sweet holiday

| X | ¼X | B'ST | DMC |
|---|---|---|---|
| ② | | | B5200 |
| ◆ | | | 304 |
| ■ | | | 310 |
| ‖ | | | 320 |
| • | ▨ | | 367 |
| • | ◥ | | 434 |
| ◈ | ◥ | | 435 |

| X | ¼X | B'ST | DMC |
|---|---|---|---|
| ☆ | | | 597 |
| + | | | 676 |
| ✕ | | ▨ | 741 |
| ▢ | | | 744 |
| ◀ | | | 745 |
| • | | ◿ | 762 |
| ▮ | | | 775 |

| X | ¼X | B'ST | DMC |
|---|---|---|---|
| ◀ | ◥ | | 815 |
| ○ | | | 839 |
| ◈ | ◥ | | 840 |
| ■ | | | 938 |
| | | ◿ | 948 |
| | | | 3072 |
| | | | 3809 |

| X | ¼X | B'ST | DMC |
|---|---|---|---|
| Ⓑ | ◥ | | 3810 |

Kreinik Blending
Filament - 002
775 French Knot
938 French Knot
Pink area indicates last row
of top section of design.

**Holiday House in Frame**
(shown on page 7): The
design was stitched over
2 fabric threads on a
15" x 19" piece of Antique
White Lugana (25 ct). Three
strands of floss were
used for Cross Stitch
and 1 strand of floss or
blending filament for
Backstitch and French
Knots. Personalize and
date design using alphabet
and numerals provided.
It was custom framed.

*Design by*
*Deborah Lambein.*

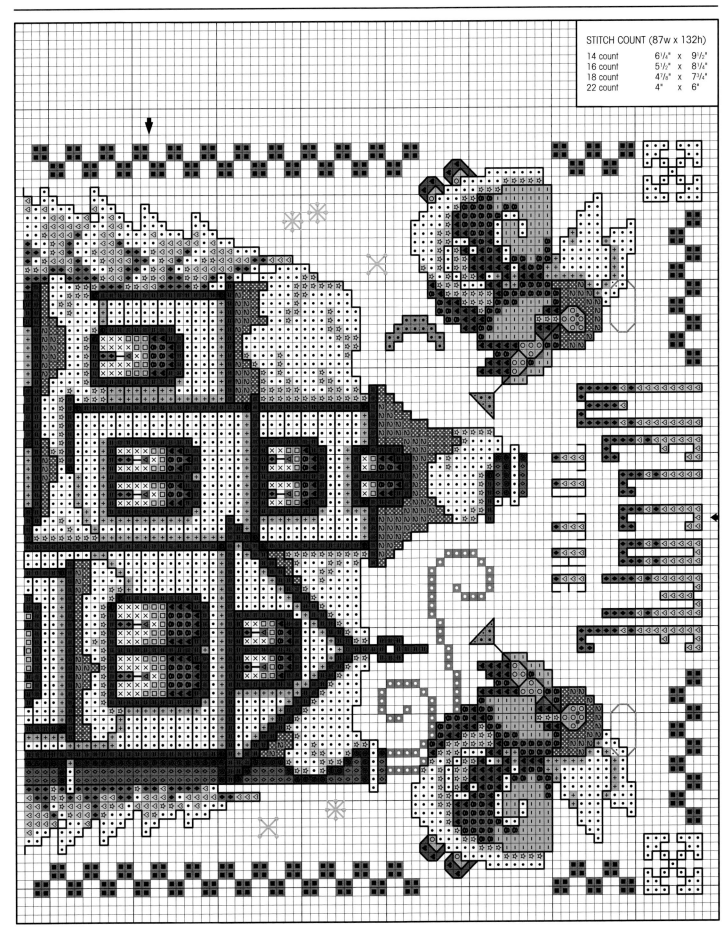

STITCH COUNT (87w x 132h)

| count | width | | height |
|---|---|---|---|
| 14 count | 6¼" | x | 9½" |
| 16 count | 5½" | x | 8¼" |
| 18 count | 4⅞" | x | 7¾" |
| 22 count | 4" | x | 6" |

# cheery christmas kitchen

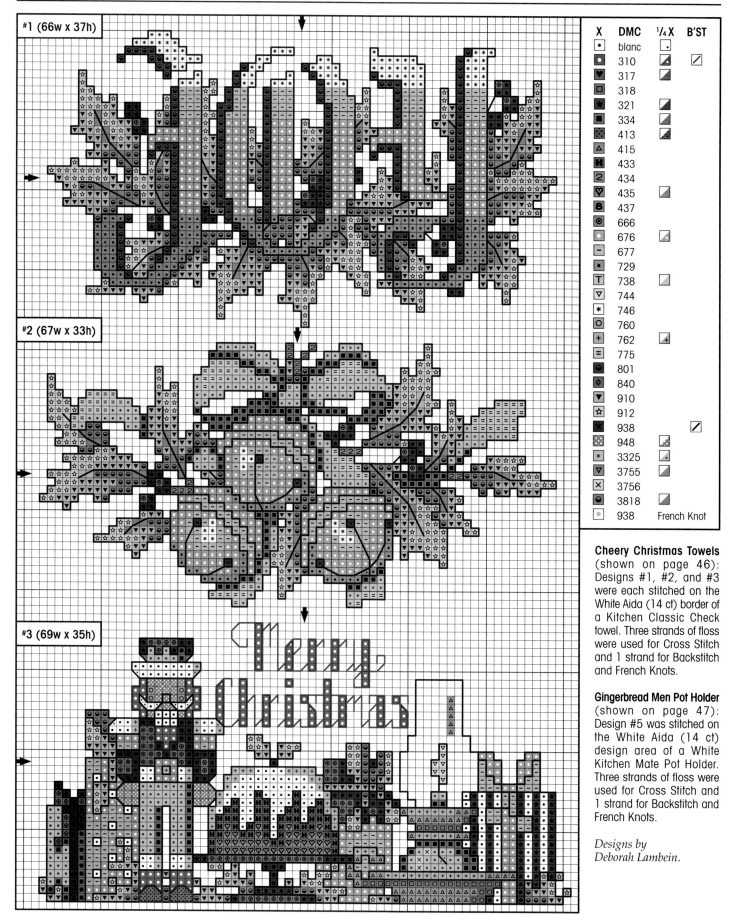

#1 (66w x 37h)

#2 (67w x 33h)

#3 (69w x 35h)

| X | DMC | 1/4 X | B'ST |
|---|---|---|---|
| • | blanc | • | |
| ▣ | 310 | ◪ | ◢ |
| ▼ | 317 | ◪ | |
| ▢ | 318 | | |
| ★ | 321 | ◪ | |
| ▪ | 334 | ◪ | |
| ▨ | 413 | ◪ | ◢ |
| ▲ | 415 | | |
| H | 433 | | |
| 2 | 434 | | |
| ▽ | 435 | ◪ | |
| 8 | 437 | | |
| ◉ | 666 | | |
| ▣ | 676 | ◪ | |
| – | 677 | | |
| ● | 729 | | |
| T | 738 | ◪ | |
| ▽ | 744 | | |
| ✳ | 746 | | |
| ◎ | 760 | | |
| + | 762 | + | |
| = | 775 | | |
| ▨ | 801 | | |
| ◈ | 840 | | |
| ▼ | 910 | | |
| ☆ | 912 | | |
| ▨ | 938 | | ◢ |
| ▨ | 948 | ◪ | |
| • | 3325 | ◪ | |
| ▽ | 3755 | ◪ | |
| ✕ | 3756 | | |
| ◖ | 3818 | ◪ | |
| ○ | 938 | French Knot | |

**Cheery Christmas Towels**
(shown on page 46):
Designs #1, #2, and #3
were each stitched on the
White Aida (14 ct) border of
a Kitchen Classic Check
towel. Three strands of floss
were used for Cross Stitch
and 1 strand for Backstitch
and French Knots.

**Gingerbread Men Pot Holder**
(shown on page 47):
Design #5 was stitched on
the White Aida (14 ct)
design area of a White
Kitchen Mate Pot Holder.
Three strands of floss were
used for Cross Stitch and
1 strand for Backstitch and
French Knots.

*Designs by
Deborah Lambein.*

78

#4 (78w x 58h)

#5 (63w x 36h)

**"Back Door Guests" Door Pocket** (shown on page 47): Design #4 was stitched over 2 fabric threads on a 14" x 13" piece of White Lugana (25 ct). Three strands of floss were used for Cross Stitch and 1 strand for Backstitch.

For door pocket, you will need a 7" x 5½" piece of adhesive mounting board, 7" x 5½" piece of batting, 27" length of ¼" dia. purchased cording with attached seam allowance, clear-drying craft glue, 19" x 25" kitchen towel, 1 yard of 1¼"w wire-edged ribbon, two 8½" x 10" pieces of cardboard, 8½" x 10" x 3½" piece of floral foam, three ½" dia. plastic rings for hanger, desired ornaments, and artificial greenery.

Centering design, trim stitched piece to measure 9" x 7½".

To complete door pocket, see Finishing Instructions, page 81.

*Designs by Deborah Lambein.*

# cheery christmas kitchen

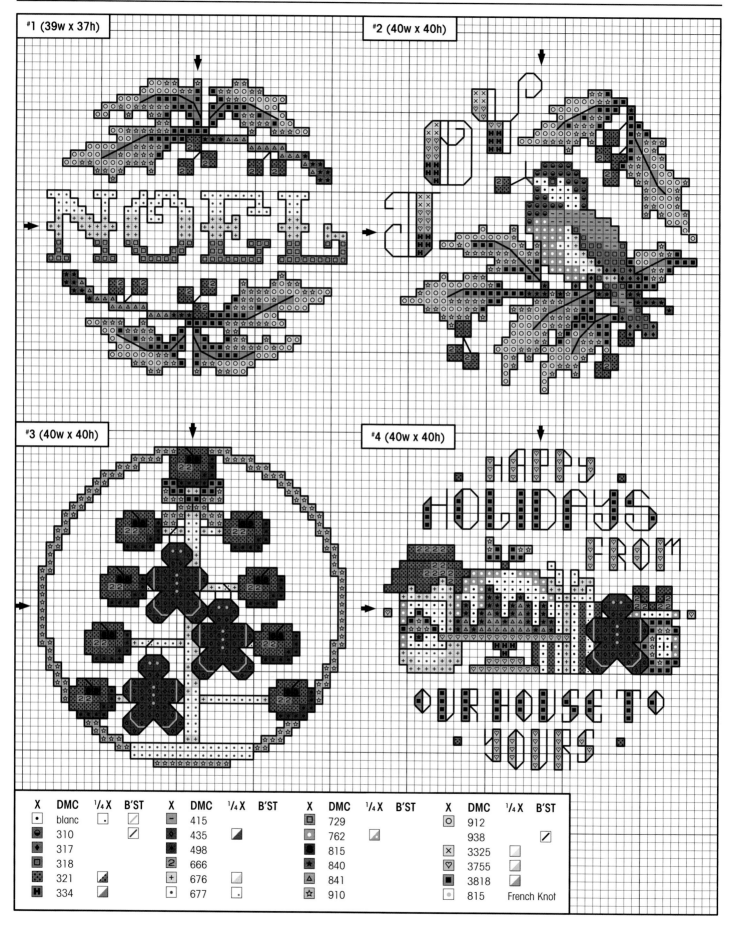

| X | DMC | ¼X | B'ST | X | DMC | ¼X | B'ST | X | DMC | ¼X | B'ST | X | DMC | ¼X | B'ST |
|---|-----|-----|------|---|-----|-----|------|---|-----|-----|------|---|-----|-----|------|
| • | blanc | • | | − | 415 | | | □ | 729 | | | ○ | 912 | | |
| | 310 | | | | 435 | | | | 762 | | | | 938 | | |
| | 317 | | | | 498 | | | | 815 | | | × | 3325 | | |
| | 318 | | | 2 | 666 | | | | 840 | | | | 3755 | | |
| | 321 | | | + | 676 | | | | 841 | | | | 3818 | | |
| H | 334 | | | • | 677 | | | | 910 | | | | 815 | | French Knot |

**Note:** Each ornament and jar lid design was stitched on a 7" square of White Aida (14 ct). Three strands of floss were used for Cross Stitch and 1 strand for Backstitch and French Knots.

**Cheery Christmas Jar Lids** (shown on page 46): Designs #1, #3, and #4.

For **each** jar lid, you will need a wide-mouth jar lid, 3¼" dia. circle of adhesive mounting board, 3¼" dia. circle of batting, and clear-drying craft glue.

Centering design, trim stitched piece to a 5¼" dia. circle.

Remove paper from adhesive mounting board; center batting on adhesive board and press in place. Clip ½" into edge of stitched piece at ½" intervals. With right side facing up, center stitched piece on batting. Fold edges of stitched piece to back of adhesive board; glue fabric edges to back of adhesive board. Glue stitched piece inside jar lid.

**Cheery Christmas Ornaments** (shown on page 44): Designs #1, #3, and #4.
**"Joy" Basket Ornament** (shown on page 46): Design #2.

For **each** ornament, you will need a 5¼" dia. circle of White Aida for backing, two 3¼" dia. circles of adhesive mounting board, two 3¼" dia. circles of batting, 14" length of ¼" dia. purchased cording with attached seam allowance, and clear-drying craft glue.

Centering design, trim each stitched piece to a 5¼" dia. circle.

Remove paper from one piece of mounting board and press one batting piece onto mounting board. Repeat with remaining mounting board and batting pieces.

Clip ½" into edge of stitched piece at ½" intervals. Center stitched piece over batting on one mounting board piece; fold edges of stitched piece to back of mounting board and glue in place. For ornament back, repeat with backing fabric and remaining mounting board.

Beginning and ending at bottom center of stitched piece, glue cording seam allowance to wrong side of ornament front, overlapping ends of cording. Matching wrong sides, glue ornament front and back together.

*Designs by Deborah Lambein.*

## FINISHING INSTRUCTIONS

**"Back Door Guests" Door Pocket** (shown on page 47, chart and supplies on page 79): For door pocket ornament, remove paper from mounting board and press batting piece onto mounting board. Center stitched piece over batting; fold edges of stitched piece to back of mounting board and glue in place.

Beginning and ending at bottom center of stitched piece, glue cording seam allowance to wrong side of ornament, overlapping ends of cording.

For door pocket, matching right sides and short edges, fold kitchen towel in half. Finger press folded edge to form one side of pocket. Using a ½" seam allowance, sew short edges

together to form other side of pocket; sew along one remaining open edge to form bottom of pocket. For boxed corners, match bottom seam with side seams; sew across each corner 2" from point (**Fig. 1**). Turn pocket right side out.

**Fig. 1**

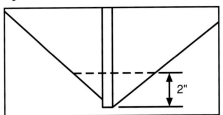

For cuff, turn top edge of pocket 4½" to inside and press. Fold cuff 2¼" to outside and press. For hanger, sew one ring to top center back of cuff and one ring to each top back corner of cuff.

Referring to photo, glue door pocket ornament to front of door pocket. Place cardboard in door pocket at front and back; add floral foam between cardboard pieces to fit pocket. Tie ribbon in a bow and, referring to photo, attach to top edge of cuff. Arrange greenery and ornaments as desired.

# BEAUTIFUL BEDROOM

*Needlework adaptation by Linda Culp Calhoun.*

74w x 108h

| X | DMC | 1/4 X | 1/2 X | B'ST | X | DMC | 1/4 X | 1/2 X | B'ST | X | DMC | 1/4 X | 1/2 X | B'ST | X | DMC | 1/4 X | 1/2 X | B'ST |
|---|---|---|---|---|---|---|---|---|---|---|---|---|---|---|---|---|---|---|---|
| • | blanc | • | | | | 433 | | | | | 801 | | | | | 3021 | | | |
| | 304 | | | | | 434 | | | | | 814 | | | † | | 3328 | | | * |
| | 318 | | | * | | 435 | | | | | 816 | | | | | 3752 | | | |
| | 319 | | | * | | 437 | | | | | 817 | | | | | 3772 | | | |
| | 320 | | | | | 642 | | | † | | 822 | | | | | 3829 | | | * |
| | 321 | | | | | 644 | | | | | 890 | | | * | | | | | |
| | 350 | | | | | 676 | | | | | 931 | | | * | | | | | |
| | 351 | | | | | 677 | | | | | 932 | | | | | | | | |
| | 353 | | | | | 729 | | | | | 986 | | | | | | | | |
| | 367 | | | | | 754 | | | | | 987 | | | | | | | | |
| | 368 | | | | | 758 | | | | | 988 | | | | | | | | |
| | 415 | | | | | 762 | | | | | 989 | | | | | | | | |

\* Use 318 for dress. Use 3328 for mouth. Use 319 for all other.

† Use 642 for hair and beard. Use 814 for berries.

★ Use 890 for leaf veins. Use 3829 for hair. Use 931 for all other.

**Holly Border Santa in Frame** (shown on page 36): The design was stitched over 2 fabric threads on a 13" x 15" piece of Cream Belfast Linen (32 ct). Two strands of floss were used for Cross Stitch and 1 strand for Half Cross Stitch and Backstitch. It was custom framed.

**Holly Border Santa Pillow** (shown on page 39): The design was stitched over 2 fabric threads on a 13" x 15" piece of Cream Belfast Linen (32 ct). Two strands of floss were used for Cross Stitch and 1 strand for Half Cross Stitch and Backstitch.

For pillow, you will need a 7¹/₂" x 9¹/₂" piece of fabric for backing, 35" length of 2" w pregathered double lace, ¹/₄" dia. purchased cording with attached seam allowance, and polyester fiberfill.

Centering design, trim stitched piece to measure 7¹/₂" x 9¹/₂". To complete pillow, see Finishing Instructions, page 84.

**Alphabet Bed Linen** (shown on page 37): The alphabet was stitched over a 4" x 82" piece of 10 mesh waste canvas on the border of a purchased queen-size sheet with 15 stitches between letters. Five strands of floss were used for Cross Stitch. See Working on Waste Canvas, page 63.

For lace edging, you will need a 125" length of 2"w flat lace and a 91" length of ³/₄"w flat lace. For wide lace, press short edges of lace ¹/₂" to wrong side and machine baste ¹/₄" from one long edge; gather lace to fit edge of sheet. Matching right side of lace to wrong side of sheet at hem edge (refer to photo), blind stitch gathered edge of lace to sheet. For narrow lace, press short edges of lace ¹/₂" to wrong side. Matching straight edge of lace to top edge of hem (refer to photo), blind stitch lace to sheet.

*Design by Linda Culp Calhoun.*

# BEAUTIFUL BEDROOM

#1 (56w x 84h)

## FINISHING INSTRUCTIONS

**Holly Border Santa Pillow** (shown on page 39, chart and supplies on pages 82-83): If needed, trim seam allowance of cording to ¹/₂"; pin cording to right side of stitched piece, making a ³/₈" clip in seam allowance of cording at corners. Ends of cording should overlap approximately 4". Turn overlapped ends of cording toward outside edge of stitched piece; baste cording to stitched piece.

For lace ruffle, press short edges of lace ¹/₂" to wrong side. Matching raw

edges of stitched piece and bound edge of lace, machine baste through all layers ¹/₂" from edges. Blind stitch pressed edges together.

Matching right sides and leaving an opening for turning, use a ¹/₂" seam allowance to sew stitched piece and backing fabric together. Trim seam allowances diagonally at corners; turn pillow right side out, carefully pushing corners outward. Stuff pillow with polyester fiberfill and blind stitch opening closed.

#2 (56w x 84h)

STITCH COUNT (56w x 84h)

| | | | |
|---|---|---|---|
| 14 count | 4" | x | 6" |
| 16 count | 3 1/2" | x | 5 1/4" |
| 18 count | 3 1/8" | x | 4 3/4" |
| 22 count | 2 5/8" | x | 3 7/8" |

| X | DMC |
|---|---|
| ▣ | 319 |
| ■ | 321 |

"Noel" and "Peace" Samplers in Frames (shown on page 41): Designs #1 and #2 were each stitched over 2 fabric threads on a 12" x 14" piece of Cream Cashel Linen® (28 ct). Three strands of floss were used for Cross Stitch. They were inserted in purchased frames (5" x 7" opening).

*Designs by Linda Culp Calhoun.*

# BEAUTIFUL BEDROOM

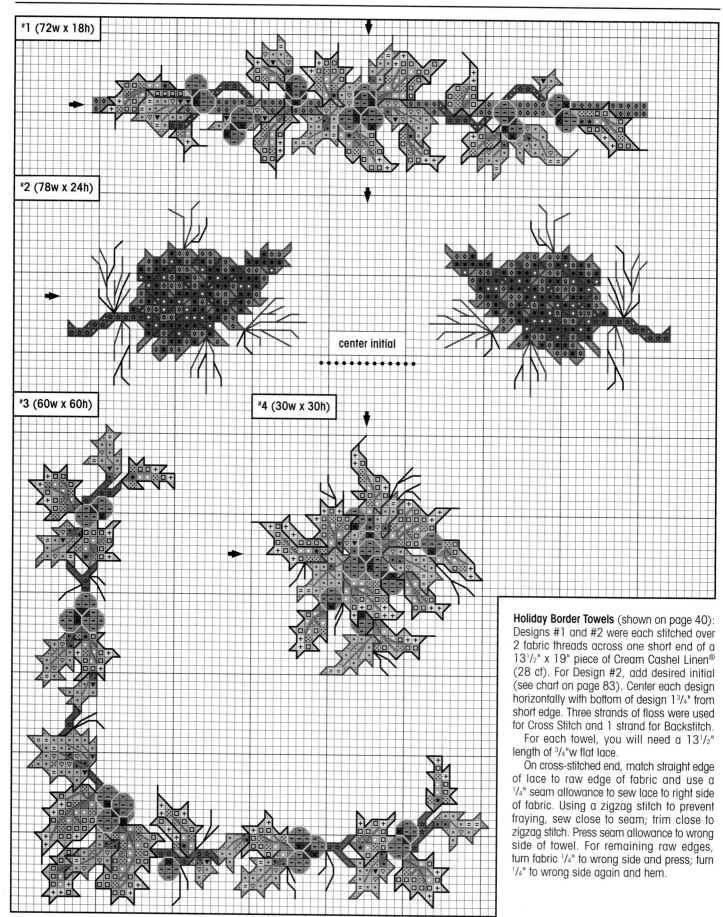

#1 (72w x 18h)

#2 (78w x 24h)

center initial

#3 (60w x 60h)

#4 (30w x 30h)

**Holiday Border Towels** (shown on page 40): Designs #1 and #2 were each stitched over 2 fabric threads across one short end of a 13¹/₂" x 19" piece of Cream Cashel Linen® (28 ct). For Design #2, add desired initial (see chart on page 83). Center each design horizontally with bottom of design 1³/₄" from short edge. Three strands of floss were used for Cross Stitch and 1 strand for Backstitch.

For each towel, you will need a 13¹/₂" length of ³/₄"w flat lace.

On cross-stitched end, match straight edge of lace to raw edge of fabric and use a ¹/₄" seam allowance to sew lace to right side of fabric. Using a zigzag stitch to prevent fraying, sew close to seam; trim close to zigzag stitch. Press seam allowance to wrong side of towel. For remaining raw edges, turn fabric ¹/₄" to wrong side and press; turn ¹/₄" to wrong side again and hem.

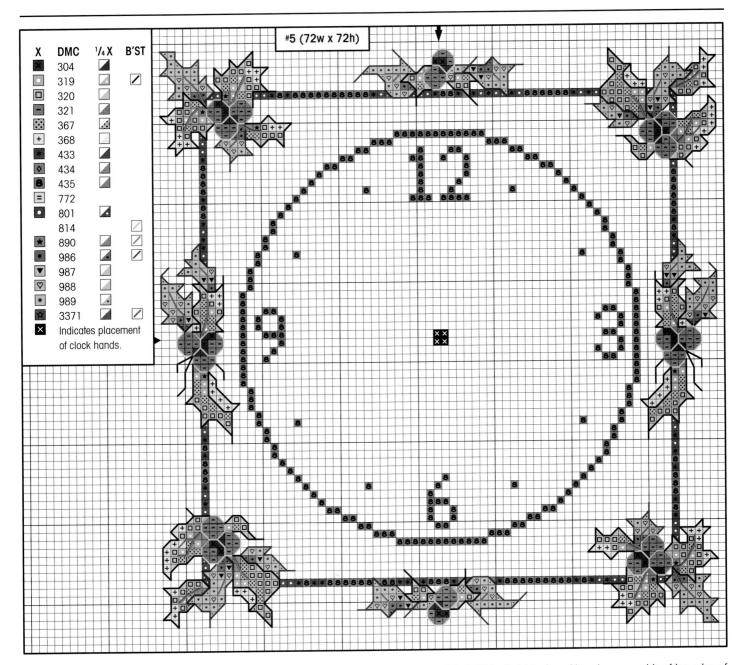

**#5 (72w x 72h)**

| X | DMC | ¼ X | B'ST |
|---|-----|-----|------|
| ▨ | 304 | ◣ | |
| ⊡ | 319 | ◪ | ◢ |
| ▫ | 320 | ◪ | |
| ⊟ | 321 | ◪ | |
| ▨ | 367 | ◪ | |
| + | 368 | ◻ | |
| ✳ | 433 | ◪ | |
| ◈ | 434 | ◪ | |
| ⦿ | 435 | ◪ | |
| = | 772 | ◪ | |
| ◙ | 801 | ◪ | |
| | 814 | | ◩ |
| ★ | 890 | ◪ | ◩ |
| ● | 986 | ◪ | ◩ |
| ▼ | 987 | ◪ | |
| ♡ | 988 | ◪ | |
| ⊙ | 989 | ◪ | |
| ✪ | 3371 | ◪ | ◩ |
| ☒ | Indicates placement of clock hands. | | |

**Holly Border Clock** (shown on page 38): Design #5 was stitched over 2 fabric threads on a 10" square of Cream Belfast Linen (32 ct). Two strands of floss were used for Cross Stitch and 1 strand for Backstitch. It was inserted in a purchased clock (5" square opening).

**Holly and Monogram Sachet Bags** (shown on page 40): Design #4 and the letter "A" from the alphabet, page 83, were each stitched over 2 fabric threads on a 9" x11" piece of Cream Cashel Linen® (28 ct). Three strands of floss were used for Cross Stitch and 1 strand for Backstitch.

For each sachet bag, you will need a 4" x 6½" piece of Cashel Linen® for backing, 17" length of 1"w flat lace, 22" length of ¼"w ribbon, polyester fiberfill, and scented oil.

Trim stitched piece to measure 4" x 6½", allowing 1" margins at sides of design, a 1¼" margin at bottom of design, and a 3½" margin at top of design.

Matching right sides and leaving top edge open, use a ½" seam allowance to sew stitched piece and backing fabric together; trim seam allowances diagonally at corners. Turn top edge of bag ¼" to wrong side and press; turn ¼" to wrong side again and hem. Press short edges of lace ½" to

wrong side. Blind stitch straight edge of lace to wrong side of top edge of bag. Turn bag right side out and stuff bag with polyester fiberfill. Place a few drops of scented oil on a small amount of fiberfill and insert in bag. Tie ribbon in a bow around bag; trim ends as desired.

**Christmas Basket Cloth** (shown on page 40): Design #3 was stitched over 2 fabric threads in one corner of a 21" square of Cream Cashel Linen® (28 ct) with design 1¾" from raw edges of fabric. Three strands of floss were used for Cross Stitch and 1 strand for Backstitch.

For basket cloth, machine stitch fabric ½" from raw edges. Fringe to machine-stitched line.

**Holly Porcelain Jar** (shown on page 38): Design #4 was stitched over 2 fabric threads on a 6" square of Cream Cashel Linen® (28 ct). Three strands of floss were used for Cross Stitch and 1 strand for Backstitch. It was inserted in the lid of a round porcelain jar (2⅝" dia. opening).

*Designs by Linda Culp Calhoun.*

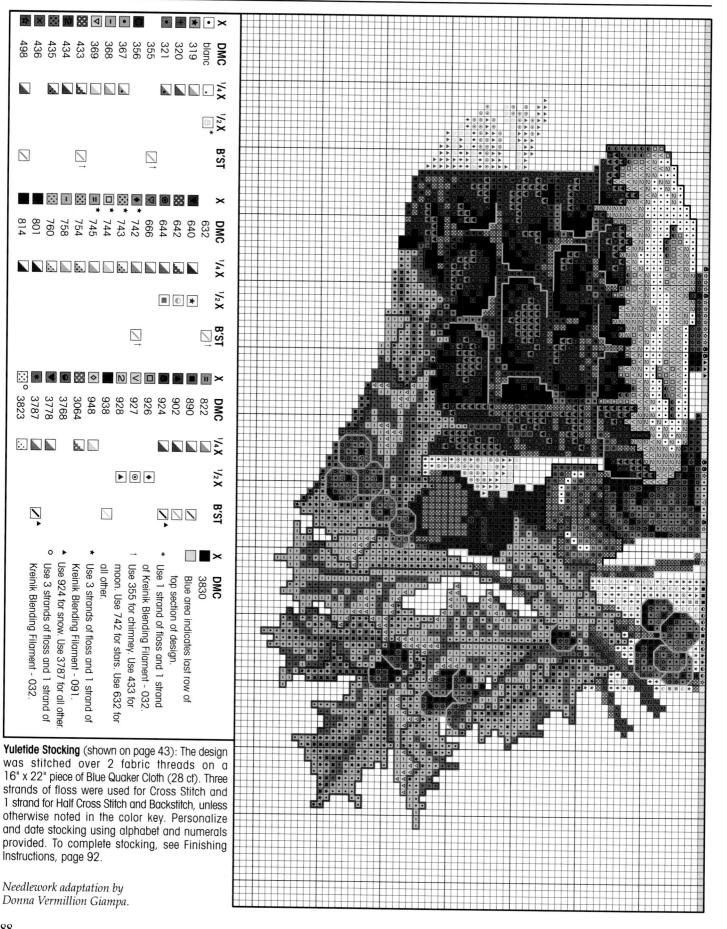

| X | DMC | ¼X | ½X | B'ST |
|---|-----|-----|-----|------|
| ✳ | blanc | ◪ | ◨ | |
| ⊠ | 319 | ◪ | | ◹ |
| ◩ | 320 | ◪ | | |
| ◩ | 321 | ◪ | | |
| ◁ | 355 | ◪ | | ◹ |
| ▫ | 356 | ◪ | | |
| ● | 367 | ◪ | | |
| ◾ | 368 | ▫ | | |
| ◾ | 369 | ◪ | | |
| ★ | 433 | | | |
| | 434 | | | |
| | 435 | | | |
| | 436 | | | |
| | 498 | ◪ | | |

| X | DMC | ¼X | ½X | B'ST |
|---|-----|-----|-----|------|
| ■ | 632 | ◪ | | |
| ■ | 640 | ◪ | | |
| ⊡ | 642 | ◪ | | |
| Ⅱ | 644 | ◪ | | |
| ▢ | 666 | ◪ | ▫ | |
| ◆ | 742 | ◪ | ◐ | |
| ◁ | 743 | ◪ | ★ | ◹ |
| ◉ | 744 | ◪ | | |
| ⊞ | 745 | ◪ | | |
| | 754 | ◪ | | |
| | 758 | ◪ | | |
| | 760 | ◪ | | |
| | 801 | ◪ | | |
| | 814 | ◪ | | |

| X | DMC | ¼X | ½X | B'ST |
|---|-----|-----|-----|------|
| ⊡ | 822 | ◪ | ▶ | ◹ |
| ✳ | 890 | | ◉ | |
| ◀ | 902 | | ◆ | |
| ◐ | 924 | ◪ | | |
| ▫ | 926 | | | |
| ◇ | 927 | | | |
| ■ | 928 | | | |
| 2 | 938 | | | |
| ◁ | 948 | | | |
| ◻ | 3064 | | | |
| ◼ | 3768 | ◪ | | |
| ▶ | 3778 | | | |
| ■ | 3787 | ◪ | | |
| Ⅱ | 3823 | ◪ | | |

| X | DMC | ½X | B'ST |
|---|-----|-----|------|
| ◻ ■ | 3830 | | ◹ ◹ ◹ |

Blue area indicates last row of top section of design.

\* Use 1 strand of floss and 1 strand of Kreinik Blending Filament - 032.

† Use 355 for chimney. Use 433 for moon. Use 742 for stars. Use 632 for all other.

✳ Use 3 strands of floss and 1 strand of all other.

▶ Use 3 strands of floss and 1 strand of Kreinik Blending Filament - 091.

▲ Use 924 for snow. Use 3787 for all other.

○ Use 3 strands of floss and 1 strand of Kreinik Blending Filament - 032.

**Yuletide Stocking** (shown on page 43): The design was stitched over 2 fabric threads on a 16" x 22" piece of Blue Quaker Cloth (28 ct). Three strands of floss were used for Cross Stitch and 1 strand for Half Cross Stitch and Backstitch, unless otherwise noted in the color key. Personalize and date stocking using alphabet and numerals provided. To complete stocking, see Finishing Instructions, page 92.

*Needlework adaptation by Donna Vermillion Giampa.*

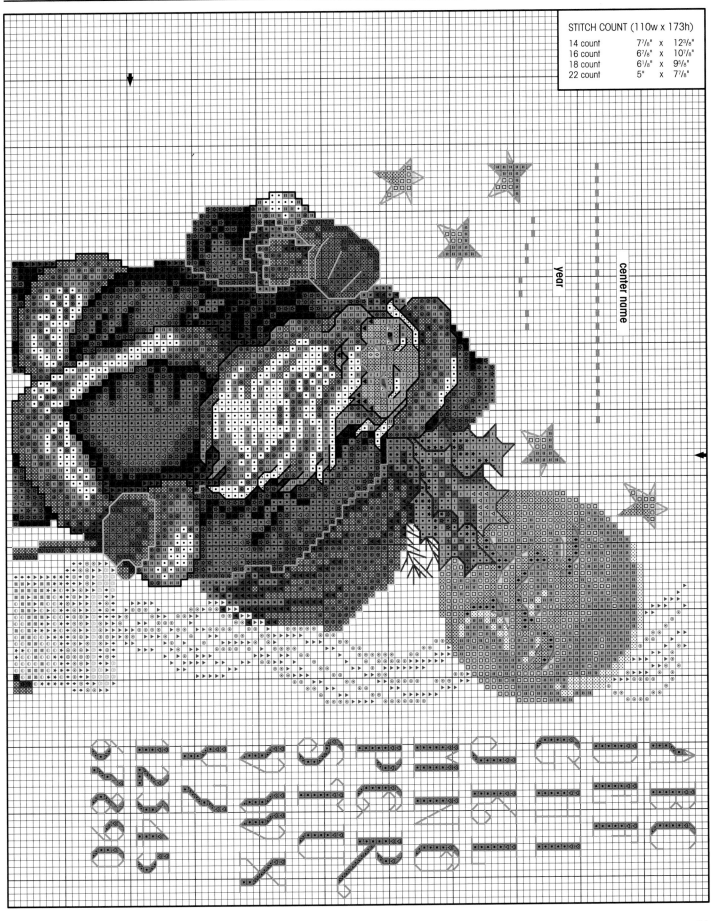

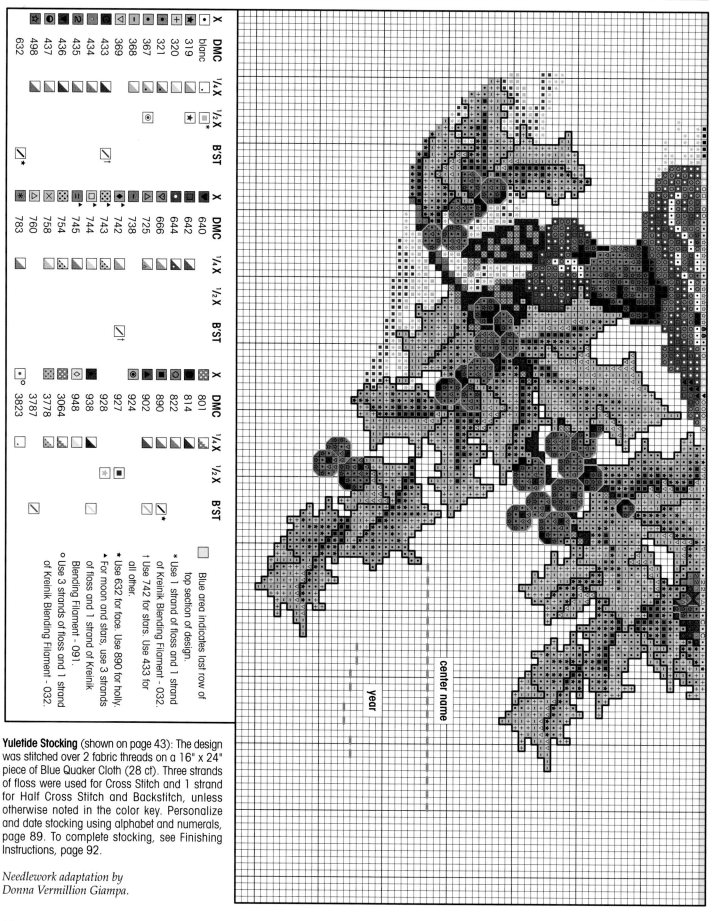

| X | DMC | ¼X | ½X | B'ST |
|---|---|---|---|---|
| | blanc | | | |
| | 319 | | | |
| | 320 | | | |
| | 321 | | | |
| | 367 | | | |
| | 368 | | | |
| | 369 | | | |
| | 433 | | | |
| | 434 | | | |
| | 435 | | | |
| | 436 | | | |
| | 437 | | | |
| | 498 | | | |
| | 632 | | | |

| X | DMC | ¼X | ½X | B'ST |
|---|---|---|---|---|
| | 640 | | | |
| | 642 | | | |
| | 644 | | | |
| | 666 | | | |
| | 725 | | | |
| | 738 | | | |
| | 742 | | | |
| | 743 | | | |
| | 744 | | | |
| | 745 | | | |
| | 754 | | | |
| | 758 | | | |
| | 760 | | | |
| | 783 | | | |

| X | DMC | ¼X | ½X | B'ST |
|---|---|---|---|---|
| | 801 | | | |
| | 814 | | | |
| | 822 | | | |
| | 890 | | | |
| | 902 | | | |
| | 924 | | | |
| | 927 | | | |
| | 928 | | | |
| | 938 | | | |
| | 948 | | | |
| | 3064 | | | |
| | 3778 | | | |
| | 3787 | | | |
| | 3823 | | | |

Blue area indicates last row of top section of design.

* Use 1 strand of floss and 1 strand of Kreinik Blending Filament - 032.

† Use 742 for stars. Use 433 for all other.

★ Use 632 for face. Use 890 for holly.

▶ For moon and stars, use 3 strands of floss and 1 strand of Kreinik Blending Filament - 091.

° Use 3 strands of floss and 1 strand of Kreinik Blending Filament - 032.

year

center name

**Yuletide Stocking** (shown on page 43): The design was stitched over 2 fabric threads on a 16" x 24" piece of Blue Quaker Cloth (28 ct). Three strands of floss were used for Cross Stitch and 1 strand for Half Cross Stitch and Backstitch, unless otherwise noted in the color key. Personalize and date stocking using alphabet and numerals, page 89. To complete stocking, see Finishing Instructions, page 92.

*Needlework adaptation by Donna Vermillion Giampa.*

STITCH COUNT (111w x 173h)

| 14 count | 8" | x | 12³/₈" |
| 16 count | 7" | x | 10⁷/₈" |
| 18 count | 6¹/₄" | x | 9⁵/₈" |
| 22 count | 5¹/₈" | x | 7⁷/₈" |

# youthful yuletide

## FINISHING INSTRUCTIONS

**Yuletide Stockings** (shown on page 43, charts on pages 88-91): For each stocking, you will need a 16" x 24" piece of Blue Quaker Cloth for backing, two 16" x 24" pieces of fabric for lining, 5½" x 16½" piece of off-white acrylic fur for cuff, 5½" x 16½" piece of off-white fabric for cuff backing, 2" x 44" bias fabric strip for cording, 44" length of ¼" dia. purchased cord, 9" length of ¼"w ribbon for hanger, tracing paper, and fabric marking pencil.

For stocking pattern, match arrows of Stocking Pattern to form one pattern and trace pattern onto tracing paper; add a ½" seam allowance on all sides and cut out pattern. Referring to photo for placement, position pattern on wrong side of stitched piece; pin pattern in place. Use fabric marking pencil to draw around pattern; remove pattern and cut out on drawn line. Use pattern and cut **one** from backing fabric and **two** from lining fabric.

For cording, center cord on wrong side of bias strip; matching long edges, fold strip over cord. Use a zipper foot to baste along length of strip close to cord; trim seam allowance to ½". Matching raw edges, baste cording to right side of stocking front. Trim away excess cording.

Matching right sides and leaving top open, use a ½" seam allowance to sew stitched piece and backing fabric together. Clip seam allowance at curves and turn stocking right side out.

Matching right sides and leaving top edge open, use a ⅝" seam allowance to sew lining pieces together; trim seam allowance close to stitching. **Do not turn lining right side out.** With wrong sides facing, place lining inside stocking. Baste stocking and lining together close to top edge.

For stocking cuff, match right sides and short edges; fold cuff in half. Using a ½" seam allowance, sew short edges together. Repeat for cuff backing.

Matching right sides, raw edges, and seams, use a ½" seam allowance to sew cuff and cuff backing together along lower edge of cuff; turn right side out and press. Baste cuff and cuff backing together close to raw edges.

Referring to photo and matching raw edges, place right side of cuff to inside of stocking with cuff back seam at center back of stocking. Use a ½" seam allowance to sew cuff and stocking together. Fold cuff 4½" to outside of stocking and press.

For cuff decoration, you will need a 20" length of 1⅜"w wire-edged ribbon for bow, 1½" dia. jingle bell, 6" length of ⅛"w ribbon for bell, desired greenery, and clear-drying craft glue. Tie wire-edged ribbon into bow; attach bell to bow with ribbon. Referring to photo, glue bow and bell to greenery. Blind stitch decoration to stocking cuff.

For hanger, fold ribbon in half, matching short edges. Referring to photo, blind stitch to inside of stocking.

STOCKING
BOTTOM
PATTERN

STOCKING
TOP
PATTERN

# youthful yuletide

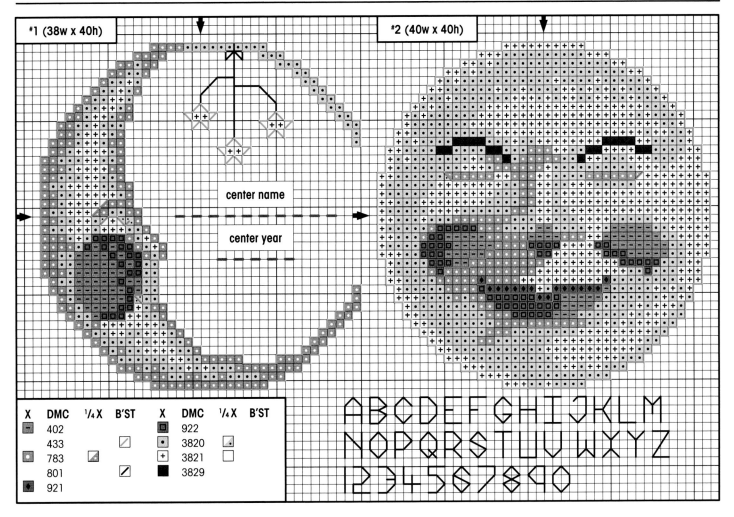

#1 (38w x 40h)

#2 (40w x 40h)

center name

center year

| X | DMC | ¼ X | B'ST | X | DMC | ¼ X | B'ST |
|---|---|---|---|---|---|---|---|
| – | 402 | | | ◩ | 922 | | |
| | 433 | ◿ | | • | 3820 | ◿ | |
| ◙ | 783 | ◿ | | + | 3821 | ◹ | |
| | 801 | ◿ | | ■ | 3829 | □ | |
| ◆ | 921 | | | | | | |

**Moon Ornament** (shown on page 42): Each design was stitched over 2 fabric threads on a 7" square of Cream Cashel Linen® (28 ct). Three strands of floss were used for Cross Stitch and 1 strand for Backstitch. Personalize and date Design #1 using alphabet and numerals provided. They were made into one fringed ornament.

For ornament, find center of each design and mark placement with a pin. Matching wrong sides and centers of designs, pin stitched pieces together.

To determine stitching line for cross-stitched border, measure out ½" from edge of design on all sides; mark placement with pins. Baste stitched pieces together along determined stitching line. Leaving an opening at bottom for stuffing, use DMC 783 floss and cross stitch pieces together along basting line using Reversible Cross Stitch (**Figs. 1-4**). Remove basting threads. Stuff ornament with polyester fiberfill and use Reversible Cross Stitch to cross stitch final closure. Trim fabric ½" from border and fringe to cross-stitched border.

*Designs by Anne Stanton.*

**Reversible Cross Stitch:** (**Note:** Bring threaded needle up at **1** and all **odd** numbers, down at **2** and all **even** numbers. Pink lines represent stitches on back. Blue and black lines represent stitches on front.) For horizontal rows, work stitches in four journeys as shown in **Figs. 1 and 2.** For vertical rows, begin at bottom and work stitches in four journeys as shown in

**Figs. 3 and 4.** Stitch **25-26** in **Figs. 2 and 4** is used to carry floss to back. Secure end of floss by carefully weaving under a few stitches.

Fig. 1

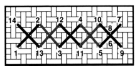

Fig. 2

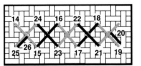

Fig. 3

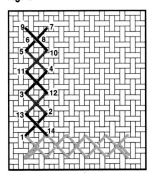

Fig. 4

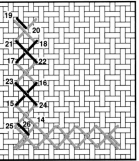

# FESTIVE FAMILY ROOM

## FINISHING INSTRUCTIONS

**Santa Collection Wall Hanging** (shown on page 31, charts and supplies on pages 68-70): For backing, cut a piece of red plaid fabric same size as wall hanging front. Cut a piece of batting same size as backing fabric.

Matching right sides and raw edges, place backing fabric on wall hanging front; place batting on backing fabric. Sew all three layers together, leaving an opening for turning. Trim corners diagonally and turn right side out. Blind stitch opening closed.

For hanging sleeve, cut one 3" x 21" piece of red plaid fabric. Press all edges 1/4" to wrong side; press edges 1/4" to wrong side again. Machine stitch pressed edges in place. With one long edge of hanging sleeve 1/4" below top of wall hanging, center and pin hanging sleeve to backing. Whipstitch long edges of hanging sleeve to backing.

Referring to photo for placement, sew buttons to wall hanging.

**Button Santa Ornament** (shown on page 32, chart on page 70): Design #9 was stitched on an 8" square of Ivory Aida (14 ct). Three strands of floss were used for Cross Stitch and 1 strand for Backstitch.

For ornament, you will need a 4 1/2" dia. circle of adhesive mounting board, a 4 1/2" dia. circle of batting, an 8" length of 3/8"w ribbon for hanger, a 4 1/4" dia. circle of felt for backing, assorted buttons, and clear-drying craft glue.

Centering design, trim stitched piece to a 6" dia. circle.

Remove paper from mounting board and press batting piece onto mounting board.

Clip 1/2" into edge of stitched piece at 1/2" intervals. Center wrong side of stitched piece over batting on mounting board piece; fold edges of stitched piece to back of mounting board and glue in place. For hanger, fold length of ribbon in half and, referring to photo, glue ends of ribbon to wrong side of mounting board. Glue felt to back of mounting board.

Referring to photo, glue assorted buttons to ornament.

**Button Wreath Santa** (shown on page 30, chart on page 68): Design #2 was stitched over 2 fabric threads on a 15" square of Ivory Aida (14 ct). Seven strands of floss were used for Cross Stitch and 3 strands for Backstitch. It was inserted in a custom made button frame.

For button frame, you will need an 11 1/2" dia. circle of 1/8" thick adhesive mounting board for frame, a 10 3/4" dia. circle of 1/8" thick adhesive mounting board to attach stitched piece to, a 10 3/4" dia. circle of tracing paper for pattern, a 10 1/2" dia. circle of felt for backing, 3" sawtooth hanger, craft knife, clear-drying craft glue, and assorted buttons.

For button frame, cut an 8" dia. circle in center of 11 1/2" dia. circle of adhesive mounting board, forming a 1 3/4" wide circular frame (**Fig. 1**). Referring to photo, glue assorted buttons to frame.

**Fig. 1**

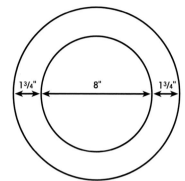

Center pattern on wrong side of stitched piece; pin pattern in place. Cut stitched piece **1" larger** than pattern. Remove paper from 10 3/4" dia. circle of adhesive mounting board. Center wrong side of stitched piece over mounting board and press onto mounting board. Clip 1/2" into edge of stitched piece at 1/2" intervals. Fold edges to back of mounting board and glue in place. Glue felt to back of mounting board.

Centering design, glue outer edges of stitched piece to wrong side of button frame. Attach hanger to back of frame.

**Santa Pillows** (shown on page 34, charts on pages 68 and 70): Designs #1, #4, and #8 were each stitched on a 10" square of Ivory Aida (14 ct). Three strands of floss were used for Cross Stitch and 1 strand for Backstitch and French Knot.

For each pillow, you will need 60"w wool fabric (1/8 yd of green and 1/4 yd of red plaid), a 4 1/4" square piece of tracing paper for pattern, thread, polyester fiberfill, and 4 assorted buttons.

Referring to photo, position pattern on wrong side of stitched piece; pin pattern in place. Cut stitched piece **1/2" larger** than pattern on all sides.

Referring to tables below, cut the number of pieces specified from the fabrics indicated.

### RED PLAID FABRIC

| FABRIC PIECE | QUANTITY | SIZE |
|---|---|---|
| A | 2 | 2 1/2" x 5 1/4" |
| B | 2 | 2 1/2" x 5 1/4" |

### GREEN FABRIC

| FABRIC PIECE | QUANTITY | SIZE |
|---|---|---|
| C | 4 | 2 1/2" square |

**Note:** When piecing pillows, always match right sides and raw edges. Use a 1/2" seam allowance for all seams.

Referring to Diagram for placement, join stitched piece and A fabric pieces. Sew B fabric pieces and C fabric pieces together to form two strips. Referring to Diagram, sew strips to stitched piece and A fabric pieces.

### DIAGRAM

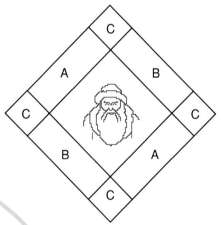

For pillow backing, cut a piece of red plaid fabric same size as pillow front.

Matching right sides and leaving an opening for turning, sew pillow front and backing fabric together. Trim seam allowances diagonally at corners; turn pillow right side out, carefully pushing corners outward. Stuff pillow with polyester fiberfill and blind stitch opening closed.

Referring to photo, sew buttons to pillow.

"O Christmas Tree" and "Joy to All" Stocking Bottom Pattern

Instructions on page 70.

Stocking Top Pattern

# LOVELY LIVING ROOM

**FINISHING INSTRUCTIONS**

**Snowflake Mitten Ornaments** (shown on pages 16-17, charts and supplies on pages 60-61): For pattern, trace Mitten Pattern onto tracing paper; cut out pattern. Referring to photo, position pattern on wrong side of one stitched piece; pin pattern in place. Use fabric marking pencil to draw around pattern; remove pattern. Matching right sides, pin stitched piece and backing fabric together. Reverse pattern and repeat on remaining stitched piece.

For each mitten, leave top edge open and use a short stitch length to sew directly on drawn line (backstitch at beginning and end of seam); remove pins. Trim top edge along drawn line and trim seam allowance to ¹/₄"; clip curves and turn mitten right side out. Turn top edge of mitten ¹/₄" to wrong side and press; turn ¹/₄" to wrong side again and hem. Referring to photo, pin lace around top edge of mitten and blind stitch lace in place.

For hanger, refer to photo and tack ribbon ends to inside of each mitten at thumb seam.

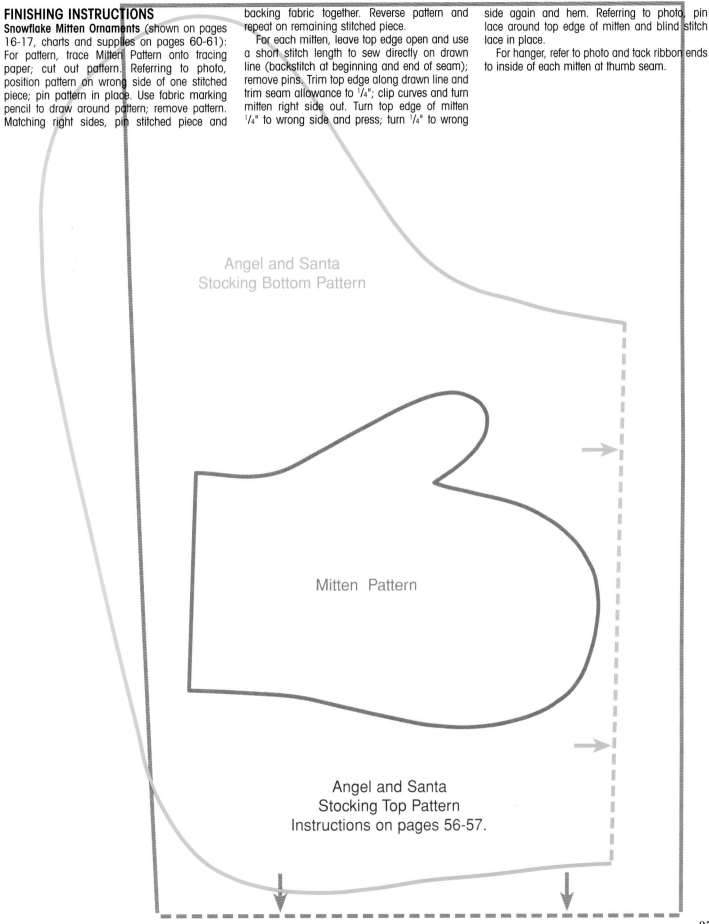

Angel and Santa
Stocking Bottom Pattern

Mitten Pattern

Angel and Santa
Stocking Top Pattern
Instructions on pages 56-57.

# GENERAL INSTRUCTIONS

## WORKING WITH CHARTS

**How to Read Charts:** Each of the designs is shown in chart form. Each colored square on the chart represents one Cross Stitch or one Half Cross Stitch. Each colored triangle on the chart represents one Quarter Stitch. In some charts, reduced symbols are used to indicate Quarter Stitches (**Fig. 1**). **Fig. 2** and **Fig. 3** indicate Cross Stitch under Backstitch.

**Fig. 1**    **Fig. 2**    **Fig. 3**

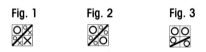

Black or colored dots on the chart represent Cross Stitch, French Knots, or bead placement. The black or colored straight lines on the chart indicate Backstitch. The symbol is omitted or reduced when a French Knot or Backstitch covers a square.

Each chart is accompanied by a color key. This key indicates the color of floss to use for each stitch on the chart. The headings on the color key are for Cross Stitch (**X**), DMC color number (**DMC**), Quarter Stitch (**¼X**), Half Cross Stitch (**½X**), and Backstitch (**B'ST**). Color key columns should be read vertically and horizontally to determine type of stitch and floss color. Some designs may include stitches worked with metallic thread, such as Blending Filament, Braid, or Cable. The metallic thread may be blended with floss or used alone. If any metallic thread is used in a design, the color key will contain the necessary information.

## STITCHING TIPS

**Working over Two Fabric Threads:** Use the sewing method instead of the stab method when working over two fabric threads. To use the sewing method, keep your stitching hand on the right side of the fabric (instead of stabbing the fabric with the needle and taking your stitching hand to the back of the fabric to pick up the needle). With the sewing method, you take the needle down and up with one stroke instead of two. To add support to stitches, it is important that the first Cross Stitch be placed on the fabric with stitch 1-2 beginning and ending where a vertical fabric thread crosses over a horizontal fabric thread (**Fig. 4**). When the first stitch is in the correct position, the entire design will be placed properly, with vertical fabric threads supporting each stitch.

**Fig. 4**

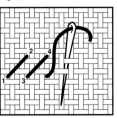

**Attaching Beads:** Refer to chart for bead placement and sew bead in place using a fine needle that will pass through bead. Bring needle up at 1, run needle through bead and then down at 2. Secure floss on back or move to next bead as shown in **Fig. 5**.

**Fig. 5**

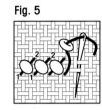

## STITCH DIAGRAMS

**Note:** Bring threaded needle up at 1 and all odd numbers and down at 2 and all even numbers.

**Counted Cross Stitch (X):** Work one Cross Stitch to correspond to each colored square on the chart. For horizontal rows, work stitches in two journeys (**Fig. 6**). For vertical rows, complete each stitch as shown (**Fig. 7**). When working over two fabric threads, work Cross Stitch as shown in **Fig. 8**. When the chart shows a Backstitch crossing a colored square (**Fig. 9**), a Cross Stitch should be worked first; then the Backstitch (**Fig. 14** or **15**) should be worked on top of the Cross Stitch.

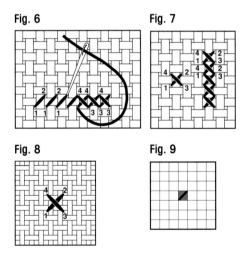

**Fig. 6**    **Fig. 7**

**Fig. 8**    **Fig. 9**

**Quarter Stitch (¼X):** Quarter Stitches are denoted by triangular shapes of color on the chart and on the color key. For a Quarter Stitch, come up at 1 (**Fig. 10**), then split fabric thread to go down at 2. **Fig. 11** shows the technique for Quarter Stitches when working over two fabric threads.

**Fig. 10**    **Fig. 11**

**Half Cross Stitch (½X):** This stitch is one journey of the Cross Stitch and is worked from lower left to upper right as shown in **Fig. 12**. When working over two fabric threads, work Half Cross Stitch as shown in **Fig. 13**.

**Fig. 12**    **Fig. 13**

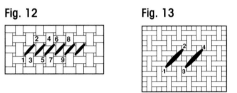

**Backstitch (B'ST):** For outline detail, Backstitch (shown on chart and on color key by black or colored straight lines) should be worked after the design has been completed (**Fig. 14**). When working over two fabric threads, work Backstitch as shown in **Fig. 15**.

**Fig. 14**    **Fig. 15**

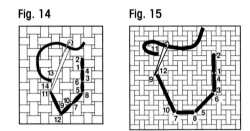

**French Knot:** Bring needle up at 1. Wrap floss once around needle and insert needle at 2, holding end of floss with non-stitching fingers (**Fig. 16**). Tighten knot, then pull needle through fabric, holding floss until it must be released. For larger knot, use more strands of floss; wrap only once.

**Fig. 16**

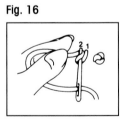

Instructions tested and photo items made by Arlene Allen, Lois Allen, Lisa Arey, Kandi Ashford, Carrie Clifford, Vanessa Edwards, Diane Fischer, Vickie S. Hilton, Diana Hoke, Elizabeth James, Pat Johnson, Wanda J. Linsley, Phyllis Lundy, Karen Matthew, Susan McDonald, Pamela Nash, Linda L. Nelson, Patricia O'Neil, Rebecca K. Parsons, Cynthia Sanders, Susan Sego, Lavonne Sims, Lorissa Smith, Amy Taylor, and Trish Vines.